THE
WHITE
TABLETS
OF
MELCHIZEDEK

A CHANNELED TEXT

THE
WHITE
TABLETS
OF
MELCHIZEDEK

THE CODES OF TRUTH

CHRISTINA RICE

GOLDEN
HOUR
PUBLISHING

Published and distributed by Golden Hour Publishing.
Rice, Christina
The White Tablets of Melchizedek: The Codes of Truth
Library of Congress Control Number: 2023910615
978-1-959513-04-9 Paperback
978-1-959513-05-6 Hardcover
978-1-959513-06-3 eBook

CONTENTS

INTRODUCTION

The deep craving for uncovering *more* in life has always driven me—more love, more wisdom, more understanding, more fulfillment. I always felt like I was looking for something deeper, even though I wasn't sure exactly what it was. That incessant hunger has been within me for as long as I can remember, and it was my essence as a seeker and explorer that kept me curious and open to any ideas or experiences that could help me find *it*—whatever *it* was.

No idea has ever felt too absurd for me to consider, and much of that stems from my otherworldly childhood experiences. I was energetically open and psychically aware at a very young age, and it was normal for me to communicate with nonphysical spirits in my room each night. I never shared those experiences with anyone until I rediscovered my intuitive gifts as an adult after having shut them down for years, eventually embracing them so much that they became the central focus of my career. The conversations I had with my angels and spirit guides at a young age, and the ones I have now, always gave me something I was looking for—a soul remembrance that satisfied that deep craving I've known for far too long.

At a very young age, the high priest Melchizedek began to visit me in nonphysical form. While there are many references to him throughout history, literature, and religious texts as a priest and king, I know him as a master teacher who wishes to help us access our inner wisdom and align with our highest truths through deep learning. To me, he is a master ascension guide. As a child, I thought of him as somewhere between an old, sage wizard and Santa Claus—with piercing blue, kind eyes and a long white beard, radiating the energy of pure love. He visited me in the form of a hologram most evenings—a white light in the corner of my room that took the form of a tall, thin man with bright eyes and an electric blue energy pulsing around him. He has always been a peaceful, loving force in my life, like a grandfather there to teach me ancient wisdom.

There are a few spirit guides I have very close relationships with as an intuitive channel, and Melchizedek is certainly one of them. He is the guide who has visually been with me the longest, through my clairvoyance—always there to comfort and guide me. In his own way, he always lovingly pushed me to be a more authentic version of myself. His presence is what kept my childlike curiosities and excitements alive. As I felt others "growing up" around me, he kept me in tune with another world of magic and divine wisdom. As I grew older, what he taught me and the way in which he guided me also shifted, calling me up to a new level of spiritual and emotional maturity. Melchizedek has always guided me in finding my truth, even when my ego didn't want to see it. He has always encouraged me to find mastery through living as the student. He has shown me the power of humility. He has taught me how to work with energy, how to strengthen my natural gifts, and how to discern soul versus ego. He is incredibly loving, but also very direct. In many ways, he inspired me to be the same.

About a year before channeling this text, I connected with Melchizedek in meditation and he requested I scribe a project for him. When I asked what it was, his reply was, "My White Tablets." I pressed for more but didn't get much else other than that they were important and I would be told when the timing was right. Eventually that time came, along with a bit more information. Melchizedek stated, "The White Tablets are Codes of Truth that will unlock ascension for those who are ready." As soon as he said that, I could see them and feel them—I just had to scribe them for him.

I sat with Melchizedek over two weekends for about nine hours of total writing time to scribe the Tablets. He spoke, which I hear through my clairaudience, and I wrote. It was pure magic. If you're reading this, then they are meant for you. The codes in this text will call forward the people who are meant to read and receive them. Reading the tablets themselves will unlock a divine knowing within you. There is a frequency transfer through reading this text that will naturally recalibrate you to your highest truth. All you have to do is notice what realigns, what comes up in your reality, and what your intuition guides you toward during and after reading the tablets.

They are meant to be both a vibrational transfer of information—as you will receive far more information than just what is written—and direct ascension codes. The White Tablets map out the frequencies that Melchizedek teaches are most important for ascension. He says that through aligning with these, the ascension process will naturally flow. This process allows us to live from a higher state of consciousness, turn on more of our spiritual gifts, remember who we really are and why we are here, live our purpose, anchor light onto the earth plane, and raise the frequency of the planet. In sum, Melchizedek shares that living these codes allows us to unlock ascension and access our next level of spiritual mastery. He is a teacher and guide here to aid us in the ascension process, and the White Tablets are his curriculum.

The White Tablets have been vibrationally transferred to many for a long time, but we are ready as a collective for them to be in written format for more people to access. Melchizedek has explained that far more people are seeking deeper knowledge and feeling that craving for more than ever before. That craving is their internal knowing that there *is* more. As I mentioned, I know this text will naturally attract those who are meant to read it. If you're here, it's not a coincidence. You're ready for something bigger in your life.

As with all channeled information, and information in general, practice discernment. Take what resonates, and leave what doesn't. My work is simply to be the messenger, and while I am endlessly grateful to be the chosen scribe for this text, it's very important to me to remind you to consume all information responsibly. This channeled text is just a perspective, and you can take what you feel is valuable from it. Feel free to leave the rest. Because this is scribed as a direct transmission from Melchizedek, you might notice the language is a bit different than what you're used to. I write down exactly what I hear clairaudiently. The guides often phrase things in ways I personally would not, not always following the rules of grammar and sometimes using words in a unique order. It's all part of the transmission. I encourage you to not just read the words—feel them.

More than the content itself, the frequency of the text will unlock something within you. It is your own inner knowing that is most valuable. You might feel tingles or waves of energy as you move through the tablets—this is the frequency getting transmitted to you on a level beyond conscious awareness. These are the energetic activations that shift your frequency and turn on soul memory. You might also feel like you need to slow down and re-read certain sections. The tablets are very dense in terms of what they can activate, so take your time with these. There is no need to rush. The first time I re-read the tablets, it took me days just to get through a few pages because of everything it was unlocking. Each sentence is like a vibrational packet of information being energetically sent to you. I felt like each line was actually a zip file of pages and pages worth of information. Watch what starts to shift in your life as you work with the text, reflecting on what it brings up within you.

Channeling the White Tablets and reading them back were profound experiences for me in many ways. As I mentioned, it took me much longer than I expected to read them back because of how much they activated me physically, emotionally, and spiritually. It has been fascinating to watch what has been delivered on my path since scribing and reading them. I have seen my intuitive gifts and healing abilities expand, I've attracted a number of new soulmate relationships, and I've released many things in my life I never expected to release. I have experienced truly indescribable spiritual activations that have transformed my life. I woke up to inner truths I had no idea I was blind to. While taking action on those realizations wasn't comfortable, it led me to a new sense of freedom. I've unlocked a new level of commitment to loving myself and to living my mission. I feel a sense of peace I haven't ever felt before, and I really do owe that to these Tablets. Although I was the one who scribed them, even I was shocked at just how powerful the transmission was upon reading them back.

I know you will receive these in exactly the way you are meant to. If you're reading these, know that the world needs your light, your gifts, and your voice. Know that you're not alone. The greatest gift you can give is living the truth of your soul. When we all do that, we create the world we truly desire—one I believe we are ready for. Your light, your truth, and your love are powerful beyond measure. Your love is healing. Thank you for living your mission.

THE WHITE TABLETS OF MELCHIZEDEK

Herein lie the codes of Melchizedek, in alignment with the codes of ascension to anchor in the truth, the highest light of all. The White Tablets of Melchizedek are herein described—the codes of truth that live within all, the wisdom and knowledge to be accessed in accordance with the path of highest ascension.

Tablet I: Truth
Tablet II: Responsibility
Tablet III: Humility and Integrity
Tablet IV: Trust
Tablet V: Surrender
Tablet VI: Love and Forgiveness
Tablet VII: Peace
Tablet VIII: Change and Maturity

TABLET I: TRUTH

To access full ascension, one must live fully in truth, as the embodiment of truth. This is the highest code of all—the code that unlocks all else, and the code that allows the expression of your divinity. To fully access your wisdom, you must dedicate yourself to the highest truth and live this from love.

TABLET II: RESPONSIBILITY

One must take full responsibility for living as truth and living as love. One must take full responsibility for their power to choose, for it is up to you to choose in each moment to live as love. It is up to you how you choose to live with the power of choice. It is up to you to choose ascension. You must take responsibility for your divinity, for your wisdom, and for your choices. It is only from a place of pure responsibility that one can fully access their ascension and creatorship.

TABLET III: HUMILITY AND INTEGRITY

It is through living with humility and integrity that one is able to consistently and fully align with truth and live from truth. To live in alignment with humility and integrity is the embodiment of divinity and spiritual mastery, as one becomes the master by being the student.

TABLET IV: TRUST

To live with higher wisdom is to trust the divinity within you, and to fully trust yourself. It is aligning with full trust that allows you to follow the ascension journey and access more of what is available to you. This code is to live from trust in your soul instead of from the fear of the ego.

TABLET V: SURRENDER

Upholding the codes of truth is to surrender the ego, is to surrender any false sense of control, is to surrender to what is the highest truth. You must release attachment to any previous identity, way of being, way of thinking, or anything external if you are committed to the highest truth.

TABLET VI: LOVE AND FORGIVENESS

The commitment to truth is the commitment to love, and living from pure love is living with forgiveness. It is aligning with the pureness of love that allows you to see the truth easily and effortlessly and allows you to act in accordance with these higher truths. It is love that breaks you free from illusion.

TABLET VII: PEACE

Peace is your guide to the highest state of alignment, where you are walking the path of love and truth. Lack of peace will direct you to where you are not living in alignment with truth, and thus where you are not aligned with pure love—your divine essence.

TABLET VIII: CHANGE AND MATURITY

To live truth is to live in the flow. To live truth is to be in the constant change of all, as this is your natural state. To commit to your truth and to living as love, you must allow for change. It is the integration of truth, of wisdom, and of the many lessons you are gifted that is maturity—the embodiment of your wisdom. In allowing change and maturity, you dedicate yourself to the ascension journey, and you commit to the allowance of truth as you know it to continue to expand.

It is through accessing these tablets that you unlock your mastery. Through living consistently in alignment with the divine wisdom that flows through you and allowing space for the embodiment of your truth, you activate the codes within.

THE WHITE TABLETS OF MELCHIZEDEK: THE CODES OF TRUTH

I am Melchizedek, Light Priest of the Most High, embodiment of Love, felt by all who wish to connect with the higher codes of Ascension. In these Tablets will be revealed the codes of ascension that are necessary for the vibrational shift of you as an individual, in turn, of you as a collective, in turn, activating higher levels of ascension to shift the consciousness that is of all, from all, within all—for there is a larger picture than you think. I trust these texts will find those who are ready to truly embody their light, truth, and love. To live as love is to embody love within yourselves, and there has been much distortion regarding what it is to live in love, for much of what you think is living in love is still living in ego, and it is through the transmission of these texts, through these tablets, that you will be reawakened to your truth.

These are the codes of truth—the codes of truth held in these tablets—to activate the truth within you. Is this not what you seek? At its core is truth. You might say at its core is love, but what is from love is truth. Truth is the epicenter. Truth is the place from which all that you desire comes. What you desire comes from unlocking this frequency within all aspects of your life and aligning with this vibration fully within yourself, and with this comes big leaps, big decisions, and a complete disruption in the ways you have been living for so long. The question is, are you willing to take the leap? To live in truth is to disrupt those who are still in attachment, still in ego, and still in the illusions of their identity and of why they are here. It creates a ripple effect that reaches far and wide, and it is through aligning with your truth that you have the most impact in changing this world—this reality as you know it—as all comes from you. And so, it requires the decision of bravery to live in your truth, and to start to dissolve what you thought you meant by truth all along.

This is the code of ascension. The code of truth. How do you start to unravel what is true and what is not? It is to start to become aware of the vibration you are living in right now. It is to start to remember that you came from the pure Source of all, from pure peace, from pure love, and anything out of alignment with that is out of alignment with the highest codes of truth. Through this text you will start to question what the definition of truth itself is, and this is the point—it is a vibration, an inner knowing, to discern the frequency rather than to define it based on the limitations of your human vocabulary. Such is the power of these tablets—they activate this knowing within you so that you can see clearly and know clearly. It is not to think, but to know. Where you have been caught in thinking is where you have gotten out of alignment with the highest truth, which is to be in knowing based on vibrational resonance, as this is your core essence. All is energy, and when the mind got in the way was when you started to get off track from living truth and embodying truth, and thus you dulled your magnetism. Can it be so that what feels good for you is in fact what makes you most magnetic? Is in fact what you are meant to seek out? Is in fact what you are meant to create?

But where does this "feeling" of goodness come from? It is time to become aware of your emotions and how you feel them, for many do not feel but rather think. When it feels good, how do you know it feels good? What does that mean? Is that from the mind or heart? Mind or body? Mind or soul? Ego or soul? Higher self or conditioning? It is time to start to peel apart these layers!

As you come in contact with the frequency of truth, you start to realize there is more than meets the eye. It is why when someone who has been surrounded by those living from ego, from fear, and from conditioning first comes into contact with an embodiment of truth, this is the catalyst that cracks them open—the catalyst for an unraveling, a questioning of how they were living before. Many simply need to encounter another option of what is possible for them to start to think differently. This is where you see that when you were choosing from the previously known options, it was based on what you knew from the mind and from this incarnation, rather than tapping into your infinite abundance of wisdom gathered across many lifetimes, many souls, and the collective consciousness. Then you realize that what you have been labeling as "truth" is far more subjective than you think.

These tablets will be direct, because clarity is love. Many of you are ready for the ascension process—you know this deep in your soul—and you have been seeking these answers for a long time. At its core, I remind you again—it is to align with truth. Start to recognize where your soul, where your body's wisdom, is telling you something is out of alignment, is telling you where something is off. You must release that which is nonresonant to get out of your own way for your highest expansion. Ask yourself, *Where am I not living in my truth? Where am I only showing part of myself? Where am I not allowing myself to be all of me? Where am I compromising my values for another's comfort? Where am I compromising my values to avoid rocking the boat? Where am I compromising myself by not seeking more deeply within myself? By not questioning what is resonant for me and instead going along with the status quo, or what those around me are saying?* It is time to be very honest with yourself. If you are not honest with yourself, you are not living in alignment with the codes of truth. This is the highest code of ascension.

If you have dedicated yourself to your highest evolution in this lifetime, where you are choosing ascension—for this is a choice—you must be ready for what will unravel within you, beneath you, and all around you. Part of your responsibility in the ascension process is humility and honesty. You must take full responsibility for yourself. There is no more room for pointing the finger at the other, for this is what has held you back all along. If you say you wish to activate your highest ascension, yet you do not want to hear another perspective, you do not want to see your shadow, you do not want to change your ways, you do not want to relate differently, or you do not want to upset others, then you are not choosing ascension. Your choice is not in what you say—it is in what you align with consistently. It is in how you show up. It is one thing to say it. It is one to think it. It is another to mean it. It is another to know it. It is another to embody it. It is another to live it.

When you do truly choose it, you will notice as everything around you recalibrates. You will start to see how all is connected, even though you didn't realize it before. You will start to notice as guides and teachers and signs and information drop in your path, for exactly what you need and what you are ready for is always gifted to you, for we truly do wish to support you on this path of ascension. This is what is key to know—it is that energies are not against your ascension. In fact, everything is in alignment with it. It is where you choose otherwise that you push yourself off the path. We are always supporting you in your highest evolution, so you can lean into the lessons, lean into the path, and lean into the love, or you can resist and keep feeling stuck. Ascension is a choice.

When you choose ascension, you choose humility from a place of love. You choose unconditional love—and what does this mean? This starts with yourself, and of course from there it flows to others. Be aware of every thought and energetic projection you have—is this fully from love and forgiveness? Where are you still in judgment? Where are you still in resentment? Where do you still need to forgive yourself or others? Where are you living in false realities? Where are you living in the past? The future? Where are you already deciding what another will do, what you will do, how it will go, and what's meant for you? It is time to move beyond your human limitations. Really, it is time to move beyond ego limitations to fully integrate what is available and possible for you. You are so much more than you know. Are you ready to step into this?

The information transmitted through frequency in these tablets is ancient information, information that has been within you and all around you at all times, but only when you peel back layers of density is it available in clarity for you. I wish to convey this quite precisely and anchor in the information vibrationally through these tablets now so that the frequency can be infused into your density in a clear way. Many of you are ready for a faster wake-up, and this will help you get out of the discomfort of straddling densities, straddling timelines, and straddling frequencies. You are naturally being pulled in this direction—you would not be reading this text and receiving this transmission if you were not ready for your next level. Remember that ascension in its purest form can happen quite quickly if you allow it, so it is key to start to release any of the beliefs you have around how long things must take. When you are straddling between frequencies, between beliefs, halfway in and halfway out, you will find more discomfort, more physical aches and pains, more back and forth in your reality, more feeling like you "do not know," and this is where I will be quite clear...

You do know. You do know, but you must be courageous in what you do know. Fully embrace what you know and live it out. What you know might be different from what another knows, and that is the beauty in it. To start to see from the individual perspective is actually how you support the collective. As you have been caught up in collective energy, there have actually been limitations in what knowledge the collective consciousness can fully access. When you start to tune into the individual and go into your own lessons and teachings and knowledge, truly anchoring in higher frequencies, more information is added to the collective consciousness, evolving everyone as a whole.

While this information was available at all times, all around it was veiled by illusions, by density, by lower frequencies, and only those who went down a very individual path and created enough space to seek it out accessed this information in its clarity. Long ago, there was a "trance," I will call it, placed on the human race, blocking many from remembering what they were here to do and why they were here, keeping them in a limited perspective of what was available. The darkness hovered over like a cloud, and those who chose the light were able to see through that cloud and move beyond what seemed to be available at that time, into this higher knowledge. But part of this "trance" was implanting programs and illusions of what was "crazy" and what was "possible"—a shaming of those who went off the path, a shaming of those who used their magic, a shaming of those who lived their divinity, as a method of pushing you out, and as a method of keeping you from shifting the planet as whole. This period offered its own lessons, but now it is time for the dark cloud to dissolve and for the masses who are ready to finally receive the codes that will unlock their ascension.

What is it to ascend? Many of you might think of it physically, but what about energetically? What it truly is is peeling off the layers of illusion, confusion, and everything that is not of your truest vibration and setting yourself free so that you can embody all possibility, exploring it all. Part of this is releasing the need to anchor into a single point of what is and allowing yourself to swim in the quantum.

Release attachment from any single idea, any single way of being, and any single thing, and you will be set free. Get comfortable with silence. Allow the divine to work through you, and in doing so, you will live as the embodiment of your truest self. Allow the divine to move through you, and ascension is inevitable. The divine does its work. When you allow yourself to embody the divine and when you allow the divine to move through you, this is, in fact, the truth of you. To live any other way is to live a lie. To live from your mind is not the truest version of you. Allow that to settle into your system and reactivate your soul memory.

There are eight White Tablets that unlock your highest Ascension. These are teachings in the High Order of Light, activations of frequencies within you from which everything else unfolds.

These Tablets are:

Truth

Responsibility

Humility and Integrity

Trust

Surrender

Love and Forgiveness

Peace

Change and Maturity

It is within the codes of each of these tablets that you will unlock the knowing of how you can set yourself free, embodying your divinity to work with the higher realms, move beyond the confines of what you have believed it is to be "human," and step into this next level of ascension. It is through these codes that you will embody truth, the highest code of all. It is from this truth that all else comes. Anything not built on the highest truth will crumble.

Recognize that as you receive these tablets, the knowing is unlocked within you, and this knowing will guide you to the tangible steps in your life that must be taken to align with these higher codes. Thus you will be guided on your path of ascension by you, your highest self, your soul self, the Source of all that is, and know that you are being supported, guided, and protected through this. You need only invoke the highest divine protection of love, and remember that your intention, your clarity, and precision with your words are all that is needed to shift the energy and shift your reality.

Where you are in fear is where you have forgotten that all is from your creation, that the energy of love and truth overrides all, and that nothing can take away your power—only you can give it away. Giving your power away is forgetting it, is not speaking your truth, is not following your truth, is acting from ego, is acting from fear, is following the crowd, is betraying yourself. There is no more time to betray yourself. There is no more time to pretend that you are anything other than divine. And what does that really mean? If you find that through these tablets, through this remembrance, ego is bubbling up within you, then it is not a true activation. This is where you must be honest with yourself.

If you notice that you think you are better than another or are judging another, you are out of alignment with your truth. That is where the activations do not truly set in place. It all simply is. You know what is "working" and what is not when you are in alignment with the truth of your soul, not your mind. It is to know rather than think. When your ego pops up, this is a beautiful opportunity to look at all remnants of what is holding you back, keeping you in fear, and keeping you out of humility. It must rise to the surface for you to look at it. It must be revealed to you so you can see it, send it love, transmute it, and clear out any nonresonant energies within you, for ascension is simply clearing out what is no longer in alignment with the vibration you are truly meant to live in.

This is an energetic process. This is a physical process. This is an emotional process. You can view this as an ego death, or as the path to everything you've ever desired. It truly is the integration of all, the infusion of love into all, the release of addictions and density that felt more comfortable to your ego but kept you in spirals of unhappiness, fear, and frustration all along. And so, what will you choose? Will you choose temptation, or will you choose love?

There are not limited chances. You can always choose. You can always learn and grow. To step onto this path is to step into the energy of learning. As you move forward with these tablets, I invite you to embody the energy of the student, a sponge ready to soak up the codes of love, ready to explore new ways of thinking and being that will be activated in these tablets but then lived out in your daily life as you encounter people, opportunities, and experiences that anchor them into your reality as a way to shift it. These tablets will set off a cascade of occurrences in your life. To be a student is not to put yourself beneath another, but to honor the beauty and wisdom within yourself and all those around you, all aspects of you, and to step into humility—the highest form, not the false version, as many of you distortedly view humility as the degrading of self. Humility is realizing there is more to explore, and if you read this text from the energy of already knowing it all, you block yourself from receiving what is available uniquely to you.

It is the way in which you show up to each tablet, it is the way in which you show up to learning new information, that tells all. How do you approach learning? To approach learning with an energy of already knowing it says one thing, to approach it with a greed for knowing more than another says another, to approach it with resentment toward the teacher says another, and to approach it with the energy of just wanting to "get it done" says another. And yet, it is another to approach it truly ready to receive. Patiently allowing. Exploring with wonder and curiosity. Opening oneself to new frequencies, while anchored in the knowing that your own intuition will guide the way to what is resonant and what is not. In fact, everything can be true and everything can be "not" based on the way in which you are receiving it, based on what you pull from it, and based on whether or not you are committed to another being wrong and yourself being right.

What if everything was true?

If you approach learning from an energy of wanting to be right or validated, you have already blocked yourself from true ascension. Open yourself to paradigms shifting and illusions shattering. Changing how you perceive the world is truly the only natural thing, and this change is really coming back into your higher knowing—which is not one static knowing, but encompasses all that is, a record of infinite possibilities and truths and the openness to explore how all can be true in one way or another. But what you are getting to the bottom of through the exploration is what is in resonance for you, from your highest sense of self—not what is in resonance with the beliefs you already have. Not what is in resonance with what your mind or ego wants to hear. Not what is in resonance with what would be easier to believe. First, you must unravel what is the truth of *you*— who you are, how you feel, where you are being honest with yourself, and where you are not. Unpack those layers to then reset the barometer and see what is a vibrational match for the clearest version of you.

Take your time with each tablet and invite in all aspects of your divine self to show you what is meant to be unlocked and shifted in relation to each. All you must do is read them, and the frequency will be transferred. This frequency transfer will activate and shift you on a vibrational and cellular level. The tablets are not meant to simply tell you—they are meant to activate a series of knowings, events, and initiations for you that will unlock your next step. Move through one at a time and allow your reality to recalibrate. There is no need to rush. Allow yourself to receive. Set the intention to drop the ego aside. Set the intention to embody the energy of a patient, curious, excited student, open to all. This is playful energy! Where you are in fear, where you are so serious, is where you block the transmission from being fully received and activated within you.

Align with the energy of ease—this will allow you to receive the transmission more clearly. Many of you are used to and stuck in the energies of resistance and difficulty. Notice where there is resistance, and then invite yourself to live in the knowing that things are meant to be in alignment with ease. Everything else is fighting against the natural state of things.

If you are living in the belief that ascension is difficult, you will find ways to create resistance the whole way through, and this is again where you feel like you are energetically straddling dimensions, and the ascension process is slower. But when you know that it is meant to be aligned with ease, then you will naturally find the "courage"—not even perceived as courage because you are in joy—to make whatever decisions need to be made and take aligned actions to continue with ease, and thus the physical body can shift more easily, the energy body can shift more easily, and emotions can flow through more easily. Align with ease.

You might notice that energies clear from your emotional field through these activations. As you receive these tablets, emotions will come up connected to energies that you are still unnecessarily holding onto from previous experiences or wounds. Allow them to flow out in a loving way. Do not keep your emotions stuck! This keeps the energy stuck and will create more dis-ease in your environment and in your body, which can specifically manifest as physical pain. As your cells are shifting and upgrading, and as you are shedding energetic layers, you might notice aches and pains, stiffness, different dietary needs, cravings, and the need for a lot of water. This can shift quite rapidly, which is why it is key to tune into your body and allow things to change on a daily basis. What worked for you once might not any longer because you are an entirely different being. Allow yourself to be an entirely different being.

You will notice that your energy field grows bigger and stronger, and with this it becomes more sensitive in terms of perception. You might notice you are more sensitive to sounds, to scents, and to others' energy. This is because your field is "turning on." You are an energetic being. Recognize that your field is alway giving you information about people around you, guiding you to the energies that you are meant to interact with—a built-in knowing of where to go and what to explore. This is to tune into, not to think about. Overthinking will stop the process. Allow yourself to rest as you need. Allow yourself to release old memories, old belongings, old ways of dressing and eating and relating. Everything will shift. You might feel the need for much more alone time. Follow this if you feel called to it, for this will support the ascension process and will help things shift more quickly. It is quite literally shedding layers of skin, shedding layers of density. Being in your own field allows you to be fully present to the process. It allows the clearing, healing, and activation to happen more easily, instead of using your energy to relate to others, to move, or to work on other things that are not in alignment with your highest ascension.

Notice what comes up for you. Notice where you are making yourself wrong for your intuitive knowing or desires based on the old way of understanding things. As you step into the realm of the unknown, as you step into a way of knowing and being you haven't experienced before, your only roadmap is your intuition, and this is the clearest roadmap. Shift your focus from getting the answers outside of yourself to receiving the answers from within. This is, in fact, faster, easier, and more accurate. It is not from your mind—it is from the record of your soul, the record of the divine, the record of all that is. Can you trust this? Can you trust yourself? The truest version of you—the divine essence of all. Remember that we are always here to support you, and we wish to give you the answers readily, quickly, and as easily as possible. If there is resistance, ask yourself why. Is this your own resistance to knowing? Is this your own resistance to change? Is it resistance to a lesson your ego does not want to learn? Is the resistance in avoiding releasing something your identity is attached to?

Invite yourself to be surprised about what can shift and change and unravel. You can align yourself with rapid transformation if you so choose. But recognize that this energetic process affects the physical, and through this you will start to truly understand that these are not really separate aspects, as you are aligned with higher planes of existence where all is energy. The way you relate to everything will shift.

Give your physical body what it needs. Rest. Water. High-frequency foods in alignment with your intuitive knowing. Treat yourself gently. Be aware of what you watch, read, and hear. Are the frequencies you're surrounding yourself with nurturing and supporting your ascension process, or are they polluting your field? These are the places where more resistance is added to the process. Be aware of the relationships in your field—you will feel the energy cords more strongly than ever before. What is feeding you? What is draining you? This is only information. As you shift yourself and your own boundaries, many of these cords will shift. What are you holding onto rather than simply noticing? For you to fully step into self-sovereignty, you must also require it of others around you—and you will start to notice the dissonance between what you require of yourself and what you require of others. This is where your energy leaks. It is to treat all with love. It is to know that all are love. It is to know that all are capable of being the full embodiment of themselves. If you are following what is in divine love and truth for yourself, it is also for another.

You will feel the push of the ego and the resistance from others around you. If it blocks you, this is a reflection of your own fears, doubts, and resistance. Notice, without attachment. This is your process. Your process heals, expands, and activates all. When you allow the projections, fears, worries, doubts, or judgments from another to affect you, this is where you are in your own way.

Be strong in truth. Align with truth. This is the highest love. These codes have been kept in the dark for much time, and now it is time for them to come to light. As it is revealed in your own life, you will see how painful it was the other way. Your light will activate the fields around you. Your ascension paves the way for what is possible. Ascension is your choice—to dedicate to highest learning from and for yourself. You are a student. You are a high teacher. It is time to reconnect with your own codes of truth.

TABLET I: TRUTH

To access full ascension, one must live fully in truth, as the embodiment of truth. This is the highest code of all—the code that unlocks all else, and the code that allows the expression of your divinity. To fully access your wisdom, you must dedicate yourself to the highest truth and live this from love.

We begin with the Tablet of Truth, as this is where all begins and where all ends. We start here to open up the space, but as we continue we will return to truth again and again. It is only through fully exploring each other tablet that the entire code of truth is unveiled within and through you. And so, what is it to be in truth? It is a rude awakening for many to learn that they have not been in honesty all along—and where this begins is with yourself. It is only through discerning truth for yourself and being in honesty with yourself that you can discern where others are not being honest with you. You must get comfortable with this energy so you can recognize it like an old friend. It always begins with you. I invite you to put your ego aside, to put your doubt aside, to put everything aside and surrender to the possibility of where you might not be fully living your truth.

This is to understand where you are not fully expressing yourself. Do you truly know yourself? Do you spend time with yourself? What are your true feelings? Do you honor those feelings? These are all places to look when you are discerning where you are and are not living in alignment with your truth. This is to be in vibrational alignment with your desires, with who you truly are, with your divine essence as love, with your essence as an extension of all that is, to be in flow—this is who you are. It starts with getting to know yourself. What are your true desires? What genuinely makes you feel at home? Which relationships are truly aligned with you, and which are there because of comfort? Which hold space for vulnerability? Being open to new experiences and new people will allow you to feel out different frequencies, different aspects of you that are brought out in different interactions through different people, and it is through this that you start to uncover more of yourself. By being in the same situations and with the same people, you are only getting to know one part of yourself, and the key is stepping into your multidimensionality.

It is true that you might not recognize the frequency until you experience it. When you get quiet and spend time alone, when you set the intention for your Higher Self to make itself known, when you call upon beings of the highest truth and love in alignment with Source to step forward and communicate with you—the more you spend time with these energies, you start to learn what it is to feel divine love—what it is to feel unconditional love. You might start to realize that what you have been experiencing on a human level simply is not it. And so, will you settle for less in your human form? Or will you hold yourself and others to this same standard of divine love, because it is accessible and available and present within all of you? This is within all of you.

You make excuses when you say you are only human. Yes, this is part of the process, but it is not to be only human or only divine—it is to be all of it. When your humanness evokes an emotion or response, the divine nature within can step forward and transmute it if necessary, can shift the vibration, can take ownership. Over time, it is the divine aspect of you that comes through more clearly, and what you label as being "only human" has been transmuted, and it is your divinity that takes its place. You realize that humanness is divine if you allow yourself to encompass more, to embody more, to hold more, and to receive more. And so, you start to spend more time in the energies of love and truth. When you are in this safe space, suddenly it becomes easier for you to truly self-reflect.

Why so many avoid truth and honesty is because you do not feel safe to face it. There is a piece of you that holds back because your people-pleasing tendencies and desire to not disrupt the status quo are your ego trying to protect you. But when you feel the true safety of a container, of a space where you are always held, seen, and loved, without any judgment, with no risk of abandonment—this is unconditional divine love—now you can relax a bit and start to be honest with yourself.

Living in truth and honesty is to recognize where you are settling for less than you want. It is realizing and acknowledging what you do desire. It is not minimizing your goals, dreams, or feelings. It is asking for more. It is knowing your worth. It is recognizing where you are engaging in white lies. Where you are diminishing yourself. Where you are not communicating clearly. Where you are hedging what you say. Where you are expressing yourself in ways that are more in alignment with others than you. Where you bite your tongue to make another more comfortable. Anywhere you are suppressing yourself. Anywhere you are operating out of fear over love. Anywhere you are operating out of ego more than soul. Anywhere you are not forgiving. Anywhere you are not loving. Anywhere you do not feel like yourself. Anywhere you are not admitting what you really want or how you really feel. Anywhere you are overly worried about what others think. Anywhere you are telling yourself you don't know, or that you can't, or that it won't be possible. Anywhere you are holding onto anger, fear, or resentment. Anywhere you are abdicating responsibility. Anywhere you are blaming someone else for your circumstances. Anywhere you are taking responsibility for others. Anywhere you are running away from yourself. Anywhere you are running away from the parts of yourself you don't want to look at. Anywhere you are not honoring your unique gifts. Anywhere you are doing what's easier instead of what brings you your highest joy. Anywhere you are not living in your highest joy. Anywhere you are not following your inspiration. Anywhere you are operating on anyone else's timeline. Anywhere you are scheduling your day or your life according to what is expected of you. Anywhere you are not consciously, mindfully living or making decisions. Anywhere you are hiding. Anywhere you are staying in the dark. Anywhere you are avoiding communication, or avoiding your mirrors. Avoiding what is no longer resonant. Holding onto what is no longer resonant. Not tuning in. Keeping yourself busy and distracted. Anywhere you know you're unhappy, frustrated, or out of alignment, but choosing to stay. Anywhere you're avoiding your lessons. Anywhere you're pushing away your emotions. Anywhere you're living for anyone else. Anywhere you're buying into the belief that there is only one way. Anywhere you are suppressing your inner child. Anywhere you are choosing "discipline" over play. Anywhere you are judging yourself or others.

What needs to be spoken? What needs to be felt? What needs to be addressed head-on? Where are you being pushed to surrender? Where are you too afraid to look? You know within you where the places are that you have yet to look. They tug on your energy field in one way or another. It might be an old relationship, part of your career, part of your daily routine, your health, a thought, a habit, or an emotion.

Where are you not satisfied?

When you look at every area of your life, and every moment of your life, are you in pure joy?

When you tune into anywhere you still feel anger, bitterness, resentment, sadness, boredom, or frustration, this is where you start. These indicate where you are not living your truth.

Where are you avoiding forgiveness? Who are you ready to forgive? Where are you engaging in negative self-talk, or putting someone down?

To align with truth is to make what is unconscious conscious, to look at everything in the light, to look at yourself in the mirror, to lay it all out on the table and acknowledge what is out of alignment with your divinity—the unconditionally loving, forgiving version of you that is here to spread their magic. You must relate to those around you differently if you are to embody truth—the highest code of ascension.

You cannot fight hate with hate or fear with fear. Address hate, fear, resentment, anger, and lies with truth. Truth, anchored in love. Communicate clearly, with love for yourself and for others. Recognize that where you are being indirect, where you are worried about perception or judgment, is the place where you are in your own way of embodying your full truth.

Who taught you it was unsafe to speak your truth? Who taught you that embodying the truth of who you are is not acceptable? This is a heavy way to live, and here we relate to the density you feel. Set yourself free so you can fully express yourself in the way you communicate, in your creativity, in the way you dance, sing, speak, adorn yourself, dress yourself, and love. Freedom comes from truth. But you cannot live out your truth without recognizing it first. What is most important is nothing tangible, but rather—the frequency.

Think of a time when you finally let something off your chest. The phrase in itself acknowledges the weight, the heaviness you feel when you are holding onto something—when you are not letting the truth be seen. In releasing the truth, you shine the healing light that shifts the world. Holding the truth inside is suppressing the energy and can lead to more distortion. Let it out—the light, the healing light that others so desperately seek. While feeling this frequency might be jolting at first, it is simply because it is uncomfortable, because it might be unfamiliar, but deep down this is what you are craving—the vibration of truth, because it allows for connection.

How can you have true connection with yourself or any other if it is not built on truth? When you do not know yourself, the truth of yourself, when you do not embody the truth of yourself, you cannot truly enter into a deep connection with another, and this is why so many do not feel seen. You must see yourself first to be able to communicate clearly with others, to allow them to see you, but also to foster a connection based on the vibration of truth. This is why so much feels surface-level for you—the connection can only go as deep as you have been willing to go yourself. Where are you expecting others to pull your truth out of you? Go first. See yourself first. Sit with yourself and honor your feelings—what are they telling you? What are they indicating to you? This is where you must surrender to your truth, for it is a powerful, beautiful force that creates and transforms worlds. Truth is the powerful force that unshackles those who have felt trapped. It is the key to releasing yourself from wherever you have felt imprisoned in your own mind, in your own body, and in relationships.

Truth is the foundation for your most grounded divinity. It is the foundation for your clarity. It brings clarity to all, which is why it is a force that jolts people, shocks people. It is the vibration that shifts paradigms and brings change to the world. It is the vibration that brings transformation to your own life.

In order to fully surrender to truth, to your inner knowing, you must be ready to know. If you do not want to know, because once you know you can't not, then you will not be open to receiving it. Underneath this is fear. What are you afraid of?

Change? Nothing is permanent. Where you avoid truth because you do not wish for things to change is where you are keeping yourself in illusion, is where you are keeping yourself stuck, is where you will feel like the rug was pulled out from beneath you when change inevitably occurs, for this is the true nature of energy, always flowing.

Commit to your truth. Commit to exploring your truth, commit to speaking your truth from love, and commit to living your truth. What follows are what you might call courageous decisions, but this is where I invite you to explore what you believe is "courageous" more deeply. Why would living out anything other than truth be normalized? How interesting is it that it is a shock to the system when people make abrupt shifts that allow them to live in alignment with their truth—moving, releasing relationships, shifting their life path—and how this creates a shock in the system of another? This is where it is highlighting a deeper desire within to free themselves in whatever ways are relevant. But this is where the entire system of dis-ease has been set up—normalizing living out of alignment with truth, and creating a culture where it is a dramatic thing to live in alignment with your truth. Why is it a leap of faith to follow your heart, to follow your emotions—the truest energy you can know—yet it is not considered a leap of faith for you to follow the guidelines or expectations placed upon you by someone you have never met, or someone who is living in their own unhappiness? This is where things are backwards.

There is no other way to move forward than in your truth. Stop to allow this to really sink in. Notice what in your energy field feels expansive, supportive, and opening, and what feels heavy or like a drag. Something within the field must shift. You cannot know truth if you do not know yourself. If you do not explore. To embody truth requires exploration. It requires going into the dark—you are the light. Bringing the light to the dark. Realizing the beauty in all. There is nothing to fear when you remember your own power, when you remember your essence as love, when you remember the divine moves through you, works through you, is you.

What are you truly afraid of? Many of you live your entire lives in fear, but you do not know what you are really afraid of. Then you realize what has run your life has been the judgments of others, projections in the hologram. It is up to you if this is how you wish to spend this experience, but there is so much more available to you. Living out of alignment with your truth and living for others is a distraction. Many spend their entire lives in this distraction, and they feel unsatisfied.

Choose joy.

It is when you speak out what you need, it is when you reveal the truth inside, that the weight is lifted off your chest. What a beautiful expression—the knowing that truth is freeing, it releases density, it offers lightness. Where you might have expected fallout in a negative way turns out to simply be the rearranging of frequencies in a way that aligns with truth, and this is how the field must be recalibrated if you are to choose the path of ascension.

Where you are committed to any single story or belief is where you might be blocking your ascension. Release it all. Be open to everything changing. It is from here you can truly explore what resonates as truth and what does not, using your own self-exploration as your barometer. The moment you get the weight off your chest—how does this feel? Notice the texture, the feeling, the frequency of truth as it runs through you, as you speak it out or act it out. It's a high. It is liberation. Start to take note of the different textures of truth, and this is how you can get more comfortable with it and start to recognize it. And then, start to recognize and bring awareness to the textures and aftertaste of holding in your truth, suppressing it. The dissonance, the bodily struggles—this will become more and more physical as time goes on. As you anchor into the ascension process, your body will be very loud when you are out of alignment with truth, because there is no other way. This is the path of alignment, this is the path of ascension, this is where everything stays in the light to be revealed. Where you are not living in alignment with your truth, your body, your emotions, and your energy will make it quite known. The question is—will you listen?

Will you set your ego aside when a truth is revealed? This is a gift, not a sign of your incompetence. Your knowing will shift and change over time. If you did not know before, if you did not realize before, it was for a reason, and the uncovering and learning is a gift for your expansion. But if you have attached your self-worth to always knowing the single truth or to always being right, you have bottlenecked your expansion. You cannot expand if you have decided you are at the pinnacle.

Many of you feel uncomfortable with the truths that are hard to swallow. That you have been lied to. That you lied to yourself. That you have not asked for what you want. That you have hedged the truth. That you have made yourself seem different from who you really are. That you don't really want to be in the situation you are in. That you want to make shifts in your life. That you are battling between two realities. That you might have been incorrect about something. That you might have been treating yourself or others in a way that was not loving. That what your ego wants is not what your soul wants.

Why are these truths hard to swallow?

What you feel is discomfort in the system, but the source of the discomfort is the energy that is out of alignment with truth taking up space in your field. When you recognize this energy and look at it head-on, this is how you learn more about yourself. This is how you are able to release it, and the discomfort also releases. It is not the truth that is hard to swallow. Truth is your medicine. Truth is relief. It is holding onto that which is not truth that creates the pain within your system—that is the source of the misalignment.

When you commit to healing, when you commit to expansion, when you commit to love, what felt difficult for you before will now feel like ease. With your new intention, resonance recalibrates. You will start to realize that what you have previously been told is normal or easier is actually much more uncomfortable.

As truths are revealed, you realize much about yourself and the world around you. You realize the games that have been played. Then you can move into conscious creation. When you realize the programs and beliefs that have been implanted in the system, you move beyond them all, and now you are free to fully trust yourself. It is the gift of trusting your own inner knowing, of allowing yourself to create your reality and anchor into ascension, rather than having it created for you.

When you choose these codes of ascension, when you choose the code of truth, this is divine protection. Truth offers divine protection. It is a powerful anchor into your highest timeline of alignment. Use the light of truth to guide your way. It is the guiding light on the path of your highest alignment.

When you follow truth, you might mistake this for following how you feel. Are your feelings truth? In some ways yes, in others, no. Your feelings indicate something. Sometimes they indicate a truth within you, but you must discern what that is. Many feelings are in fact a reaction to what creates discomfort in your system, and so you must ask what this discomfort is about. Is it somewhere that your ego was triggered? Or is it truth wanting to be seen? The key is to not take emotions as "truth" based on their surface-level labels and your surface-level perception of them, but to tune in and identify where the emotions are coming from and what they are really indicating. When you are exploring this, anchor into your divinity, and anchor into your essence as love. When you discern from this place, the truth is made known.

Where you hedge your truth is where you are not in truth. Where would you rather stay in illusion? This is not truth. It might feel vulnerable to allow the truth to be fully seen, yet this is what you crave so deeply. What so many of you crave is also what you are most afraid of. To fear it does not fully allow it. Do you wish for others to see your truth? You must first see it yourself. Do you wish for others to connect with you at the frequency of truth? You must first embody this. When you crave to be seen or known, are you willing to do the same? Where are you not acknowledging the truth of how you are feeling, the truth of vibrational resonance or not, the truth of how someone's actions are showing who they choose to be?

People-pleasing is out of alignment with truth. This creates dis-ease in the system. To come from love is how we truly support and love others, and self-compromise is not love. To people-please is to transfer an inauthentic energy to others, and this is not the energy transfer most of you mean to engage in when you wish to show love.

Many of you get caught in stories. You get caught up in how to say it and how to know. These are all ways you distract yourselves from what is most natural for you—truth. Notice where what is false, what is illusion, is all around you. This is how that vibration became embedded within your system— mainstream media, modeled relationships, food, marketing— what is in truth? It takes a clear eye to see it. It takes a pure energy to know what is truth! To follow it! That purity is within you. That purity is your divine essence that nothing can shake. It cannot be taken. Commit to releasing distortion. When you commit to this, you receive the truth of love. The truth of healing. The truth of your unique gifts. The truth of relationships.

The decision to commit to living in your highest light will align you with your truth. Once you set your intention and become aware, things will stick out to you. You will notice incongruences. You will notice where energy feels dense, heavy, or stuck. The signs are all around you and within you, but you must decide you are ready for them. You cannot move forward on your path of ascension if you do not align with the highest code of truth. It is this code that allows everything else to unravel. If you are not willing to look at all of yourself, if you are not willing to let all of your light be seen, this is where you are in your own way. If you are unwilling to release that which is tied to your ego, if you are unwilling to release what is keeping you in illusions, if you are unwilling to release what is keeping you out of alignment with truth, this is your choice. If that is your choice, your Highest Self will push you on the path of ascension, and you will be resisting, and you will not feel comfortable. This code allows for your greatest comfort in this process, contrary to what you might think.

Let the illusions go. Let the distortions go. Open yourself to what wants to come through. It is your addiction to controlling things that keeps you exhausted. Your addiction to the image others might see. Where you are living for others. Where you compromise yourself and your highest divinity. Your soul chose this incarnation to express its unique frequency and to express its purest gifts. It is a betrayal of self to not live the truth of who you are. It is a betrayal of self to not explore where you are out of integrity, because this is how you see where you can step into the energy of truth, the purest vortex of love that creates rapid shifts and transformation. Ascension is alignment with truth in all its forms.

If you commit to nothing else, let it be truth. Truth will carry you to your highest joy and to your greatest expansion.

Approach the world with curiosity. What if nothing is as it seems? *What if I know nothing, and now I uncover the truth of myself?* Approach yourself with curiosity. *What are my truest desires, and does my reality align with this?* If not, then a change must be made.

Truth has been your greatest block, and now it will be your greatest gift. Your world has been out of alignment with truth for quite some time, but you will be able to turn everything on its head positively the sooner you jump into living your truth. Release needing to understand what is subjective and objective. These are understandings that distract you from understanding what it is—a vibration. Frequencies are not rationalized. You need not rationalize what makes the color red red, and what makes the color blue blue. In fact, you do not know that what you think is objectively "blue" is the same tone another sees as blue. Allow yourself to move through the ascension process by tuning into vibrational resonance. When you are comfortable exploring truth within yourself, honoring truth within yourself, living truth as yourself, now you are able to easily discern truth in your relationships and truth in external experiences. But it starts with you. When you feel the frequency, it is to recognize the frequency. This is tuning into your inner knowing. Divine truth isn't rationalized. It isn't explained. It is felt. It is known. It is unmistakable.

When you align with truth, more truth comes to you. When you anchor into honesty and live in honesty, more honesty comes your way. When you wish to uncover the truths of your reality, when you wish to uncover the truths of love, when you wish to uncover the truths of yourself, when you wish to uncover the truths of ascension, when you wish to uncover truth in itself, you must live in truth first. You must live from honesty always.

When you are steadfast in honesty from a loving place, there is no other way the energy can flow but for your entire reality to align with honesty and for truths to be revealed again and again. All will be seen through the eyes of truth. The answers you seek will come through clearly and effortlessly because you have calibrated your field to resonate with truth. Align your field. Anchor in your intention. This is in how you live. Be honest. Be open to honesty. How you receive truths from another, how you receive honesty from another, will be a direct indication of how you will receive honesty and truth from yourself, from the divine, from your Highest Self. If you do not receive truths well, how can you expect truths to be revealed effortlessly to you? If you do not receive truths well, perhaps you are not fully aligned with honesty yourself. Otherwise, the frequency would be lovingly and easily received.

Truth is a road of white light—protecting you, guiding you, and shining a light on your divinity.

Truth is the road that is ascension.

TABLET II: RESPONSIBILITY

One must take full responsibility for living as truth and living as love. One must take full responsibility for their power to choose, for it is up to you to choose in each moment to live as love. It is up to you how you choose to live with the power of choice. It is up to you to choose ascension. You must take responsibility for your divinity, for your wisdom, and for your choices. It is only from a place of pure responsibility that one can fully access their ascension and creatorship.

The second code is responsibility. This is responsibility to the truth, and responsibility to yourself, for yourself. This is taking ownership of that which is yours—that which is in your energy field. This is being responsible for your energy, your actions, and your choices—how you choose to move through this reality. This is taking responsibility for your own path of ascension, not hoping someone else will do it for you. It is recognizing your power as the creator. It is living as the divine being that you are. This is your responsibility. It is your responsibility to take action knowing that the divine moves through you, as you. If you are to unlock your gifts, your higher knowing, and your ascended self in its purest form, you must first take responsibility.

Where do you feel that you are a victim to life or its circumstances? This is where you are out of responsibility. This does not mean you are responsible for everything that occurs or for everything that comes your way, but that you are responsible for your response, for the energy you move forward with, and for whether you infuse love or fear into the situation. It is taking responsibility for how you are showing up, and where you say you want one thing but do another. Notice where you say that something or someone isn't letting you, isn't allowing you, or is keeping you stuck, and where you feel you are depending on another's choice. There is another way. When you are fully anchored into self-responsibility, you see more options. You see more choices.

In ancient times, when more were fully anchored in their power, had mastered their spiritual gifts, and used them more readily in this dimension, they were fully embodied in self-responsibility. It is when you forget responsibility, when you put it on someone else, that you are quite literally giving your power away. In fact, in ancient times some had so much responsibility that their egos started to take over in the way of pride, and some of their innate power led to chaos. This led to an imbalanced form of "responsibility" that manifested in its wounded state.

Taking responsibility in a grounded, loving energy is where you will unlock more codes in your life and access easier solutions. This is where the solutions drop in easily, and you are no longer caught in "problems." It is where you are in creatorship, understanding that you have the pen and get to write the story. Where are you not taking responsibility? How can you take more responsibility for your thoughts, your life, or your situation?

When you anchor into responsibility, you will see the aligned actions and energetic shifts necessary to create what you want. It is seeing the changes with bravery and honor that allows you to immediately step into them. But avoiding responsibility is an easy way to stay in the realm of "not knowing" what you do know, or of not taking action—in this way, self-sabotaging your progress and path to the higher realms. When you take full responsibility for yourself, you see where you are out of alignment with your truth, and you will be guided to people, situations, and opportunities that will support you in anchoring into your highest truth. From this place of self-responsibility—full responsibility for your energy—you will follow these opportunities for learning. But when you do not move forward or take action in alignment with these shifts—this is where you are not maintaining responsibility.

What do you believe you are responsible for, and what do you believe you are not? Most of you are living from the belief that you are responsible for what you need not be, and not responsible for what you need be. You are responsible for yourself, as the co-creator of your reality, where you have infinite choices. You are not responsible for another.

To have free will is a responsibility. This has gone awry many times throughout history. It is one of the greatest responsibilities of your incarnation—it is from this that you create. And so, what do you choose to create? From what energy do you choose to create? Those who choose to use their free will from ego, from greed, from anger, or from hate create more of the same, and the repercussions are seen and felt by all around. Those who choose to use their free will from love, from peace, from joy, from truth, and from alignment create more of the same, and the repercussions are seen and felt by all around. Those of the former are felt quite intensely—as a way for the energy body to remember and for you to learn from those lessons, whether they be related to your actions or another's. The question is—are these lessons truly learned?

Take responsibility for the lessons you can learn. These are not only from your own experience, but from that of those around you. In fact, this is how you add more knowledge to your soul's record and to that of the collective consciousness—learning from all experiences in your field whether or not they are your "own." If you have to live out every lesson in your individual incarnation, you will experience only a fraction of the evolution that is available to you compared to if you allow yourself to deeply learn the lessons you are able to witness as well. Lessons are all around you. When you live in responsibility, you take note of what you can learn from, and you dive into it. You do not ignore or bypass. You take responsibility for your highest evolution.

Ascension is a responsibility. You incarnated at this time for a reason. Ascension unlocks deeper levels and layers of knowing, of meaning, of gifts, and of abilities. It is with these greater abilities and this greater knowledge that you must use discernment in what you share and how you share it. Be careful of your ego coming through—wishing to share before it is time, to impress what you have uncovered upon others when it might not be the time. Where are you trying to push the timing? In what ways are you looking to prove? Is your ascension about you, or what others think of you? This is where you must take responsibility for your ego, and this is how you take responsibility for your free will. If your ego is informing how you use your free will, you will be reactive, and you will be feeding low frequencies with more of the same. The responsibility is to take care of your ego, to be aware of it, to soothe it, and to love it, but to consciously choose to use your free will from the guidance of your soul, as your divine self.

As you unlock more of your abilities, as you realize the power within you, as you realize your ability to create worlds, to shift your reality more quickly than you ever realized, as you realize your ability to shift energy and thus impact those around you, you must be anchored into pure responsibility of the highest love. Responsibility anchored in love, in truth, from the essence of love—the purity and integrity of your soul. As you unlock more of these gifts, you will feel temptation arise. It is not to avoid situations that feel heavy or tempt the ego, but to face them head-on and be firm in the knowing that you are the embodiment of love, and that simply because a temptation is available does not mean you will falter in remaining anchored in responsibility. This is honor.

These are the highest codes of love and truth, the codes of ascension. Seeing the temptations in the darkness, and choosing love. Choosing to infuse the situation with love, and to come from your heart. Choosing your heart over your ego. Seeing the bigger picture. Knowing that instant gratification lasts for a fleeting moment, and that the joy of your soul endures the test of time. The joy of your soul, alignment—these are expansive, powerful energies. The way to continue to grow your spiritual mastery—your energetic mastery—is to face moments where there is temptation of the ego, temptation to prove yourself, to compare yourself, to meet a low-frequency energy with another low-frequency energy, and to instead choose love and soul. This requires awareness—mindfulness in each moment of your thoughts, your intentions, and the vibration of each choice and decision. You will come to understand the power of your words and your thoughts. If every word, every thought, was thrown like a dart, would you choose them differently?

This is where I will challenge you, beloved, to remember that you do choose your thoughts, and you choose your words. It is where you're caught in automatic processing that you have become unconscious, that you have given in to external programming rather than the truth of your soul. As you are more mindful and conscious, you tune into the voice of your soul, you embody your essence as the divine, and you speak and think accordingly. It seems to all slow down, but through this it all speeds up. As you slow down moment to moment, as you are conscious in your embodiment of your divinity, this is how you create rapid transformation and shifts all around you, as you are not living by the laws of the lower realms but rather those of the higher states of being. It is with love that I share this with you. Remember that nothing can get you off track other than making a choice that is not in alignment with your truth, and you will feel the discomfort of this. You know that it does not feel good in your system, in your field, when you think, speak, or act from low frequencies. It is you who receives the most uncomfortable part of this, because it is not in alignment with your truth.

Be responsible with your gifts. Be responsible with your mastery. You can create dark as easily as you can create light. You can create light as easily as you can create dark. As you start to ascend, as you uncover the secrets (as you perceive them to be) of this universe, of your essence, as it all unravels, I invite you to ask yourself how you are being responsible with your power, with your gifts, and with this knowledge. How that looks will be different for each of you, as each of you has a unique role to play. The responsibility is to align with the mission. In this incarnation, what is the divine mission to be carried out? Are you anchored into this, or are you getting distracted and thrown off track by all the noise around you? Part of the responsibility of anchoring into your divine mission and completing your divine mission is tuning out the noise.

As more and more of you anchor light onto the planet, there will be more and more noise in the field to attempt to distract you, to attempt to confuse you, and to attempt to get you off track. You are stronger than this. You are more powerful than this. You are clearer than this and wiser than this. This power, this strength, this clarity in knowing does not come from a place of ego. It is an inherent confidence, perhaps a quiet confidence, that is a more powerful force than any other, because love dissolves all illusion. Love dissolves any lower frequencies looking for more fuel. Love is the most powerful healer that shifts worlds, and truth is the foundation of pure love. And so, as you anchor into truth, responsibility becomes clear. What is your responsibility, and how do you live with this responsibility?

It is one of the deepest truths of ascension and spiritual mastery that you must be responsible, as there have been important reasons for keeping quiet much of the information being revealed to you now. You can see how emotion and ego influence humans to act in accordance with these lower frequencies, and how they have easily fallen into this trap before. And so, it was not wise to relay the information clearly, but rather wait for those who walked the path to seek it out and align with their codes of truth, love, and responsibility. From there, they could fully receive it. As things have shifted, more of you are ready for this responsibility. You do not give a child scissors if they are not yet ready to be responsible with them, but there comes a time when they are ready to learn how to use the scissors responsibly, and you honor this time. And so, these codes can be revealed, but you must be honest with where you are taking responsibility and where you are not.

If you knew you were being given the most sacred, precious treasure of all, how would you treat it? With care. With love. With responsibility. This is how you must treat the codes that are coming through, the gifts that are coming online, and the love that you are receiving—as the most precious treasure of all. You wouldn't throw it around and act as though it doesn't matter. It is prioritized, it is taken care of, it is revered as the divine treasure that it is. Where are you treating this information as something to show off and get ahead with, or as something to toss around in the air for others to see? This is where you are not being responsible. Treasure it. Care for it. Learn how to polish it and how to protect it, and act responsibly in accordance with this. It is a check to your ego, a check to your mind, to fully anchor into responsibility. You are ready for this.

Part of this responsibility is regulating what you allow in your field. Audit all of the frequencies you allow in. You might notice some resistance to this. Resistance to releasing old relationships, old ways of eating, and old ways of doing things. These are often rooted in addictions. To fully be in responsibility, you must release the addictions that are fuel for your ego, that are fuel for the lower frequencies in your world, that are the direct blocks to your spiritual mastery. The truth is that you need nothing in the realm of the material to achieve all of the happiness in the world and to step on the path of spiritual mastery. In fact, when you have committed to the path of ascension, and you cling so desperately to these addictions, to these material possessions, don't be surprised if it feels as if they are ripped away from you. This is to show you that they are not real at all. This is for your protection. When you are so happy and so comfortable sitting in an empty room with silence, then you know peace. Then you know responsibility. Then you feel enlightenment.

It is not a requirement to release it all, but to understand your relationship to that which is around you. To what do you cling? Where are you in a desperate, clingy energy? This is resistance. Realize that it has always been within you—all the power, and all the love. When you realize this and you feel the instantaneous vibrational shift as things instantly unlock for you, the code of honor is to be responsible with this gift. If you were guarding the most precious treasure of all, would you not be responsible with whom you allow to be in its room? With whom you allow to hold it? You would be precise with whom is allowed to access its energy. This is the level of responsibility you must step into in order to fully embody this code and unlock your next step in ascension. It is true responsibility for yourself, for your field, for guarding the codes of wisdom, for protecting the codes of ascension, for their embodiment—this is the level of responsibility you must have for yourself and your energy field, as the beautiful treasure that you are. As the divine embodiment that you are. When you love another so dearly, so deeply, and you would do anything to protect them, you only allow what is in their highest alignment to enter their field. You must treat yourself the same. Uphold the same standard of integrity in your field.

How are you showing responsibility for yourself? How are you showing responsibility for your ascension process? From here you grow into spiritual maturity and spiritual mastery. It is not a game. It is not a competition. There is nothing to compare to, for that is an illusion of separation. Recognize that your ascension is that of all others, that they are a reflection of you, that this path is for the love of all, beginning with you as an extension of the divine, and allowing others to be on their journey in the way that is for their highest and best. And so, you must take responsibility for your lessons. You must take responsibility for your field. You must treat yourself and your spiritual enlightenment, your gifts and knowledge, as the divine treasures that they are. This is respect for yourself, for the divine, for all—to see the beauty and the love in yourself and of all around. Without respect, there is no responsibility.

Do you fully respect yourself? What in your life would change if you were to align with full respect for yourself, and full respect for all others? It is one thing to say you respect yourself, and it is another to live it. These are quite different. Many say it but do not live it. Again, here you find a deeper truth. Is what you are saying aligning with how you are being? If you can be honest about how you do not respect yourself, and then make aligned changes, you unlock your next step in ascension. If you can be honest about how you do not respect others, and then make aligned changes, you unblock your ascension—for it is all the same.

Deep respect is seeded from divine love. When you live as love, respect is effortless. It is your new automatic way of being. Where you are not in respect is where you are not living as love. It is where you are not taking full responsibility for yourself. As you align with full responsibility, more gifts and more knowledge will enter your field and will activate within you. Many wonder why some have unlocked certain codes and others have not. The answer lies in the question—what can you be responsible for? This is not a judgment, but rather a reflection of the frequency and openness of your field. Where you are not responsible is where the field dampens, contracts, and holds a certain heaviness—where the door is blocked. Responsibility is like opening your arms wide open to love.

When you are fully aligned with responsibility—not just saying it, but living it and being it—you will receive more, as these higher codes of ascension will be a vibrational match for you. In alignment with this, you anchor into deeper spiritual maturity and upgraded ways of moving through the world and connecting with other entities. Living divine wisdom. This responsibility is where you remember your power and use it with love, and where you release all illusions that another person or a certain circumstance can keep you stuck. The perspective shifts to the understanding that all is opening your field to more knowledge, wisdom, and greater responsibility. You were gifted it because you are ready to hold more responsibility. This is bringing the power back to you, and living that power with love, humility, and integrity.

It is time to take responsibility.

TABLET III:
HUMILITY
AND INTEGRITY

It is through living with humility and integrity that one is able to consistently and fully align with truth and live from truth. To live in alignment with humility and integrity is the embodiment of divinity and spiritual mastery, as one becomes the master by being the student.

We build upon truth and responsibility with humility and integrity. What is it to be in humility and integrity? Again, this is a frequency that is felt and known on a soul level to be understood. Integrity is alignment with truth, is resonance of actions, thoughts, words, and choices, all together, and resonant with love—with truth. To anchor into integrity is to honor yourself, is to respect yourself, is to see yourself as the divine being that you are, is to live this out, and is to see the divinity in all others—in all around you. This is simply a perspective shift. To live in integrity is to live in truth, for nothing else feels like full alignment. This is to honor the truth of who you are, and your truest frequency. Anywhere you feel you are not being your truest self, where you are out of alignment with your mission, where you are not living your joy, where you are not living your fullest expression as love, this is not in integrity. Be yourself through and through.

Who, in fact, are you? Divinity! Love! Truth! Remember this within yourself. It is allowing this, the truth of who you are, to come forward, to crowd everything else out, to transmute everything else, to heal anything that is not in alignment with it. To live in integrity is to own the truth in each moment. It is not to never make "mistakes"—for what you perceive to be mistakes are experiences that were contracted for your highest evolution and highest learning. These are not mistakes. If they were mistakes they would not happen. While a piece of you might feel upset that it happened, this is not the highest part of you, which knows that all is meant for your highest learning. When these experiences occur, it is an opportunity to learn to embrace the lesson, to move forward with love, to forgive, to make amends, and to infuse love and respect into the situation. This is the healing. This is the ascension.

Part of your ascension to higher levels of consciousness, to higher ways of being, to unlocking your spiritual mastery, is to have experiences such as these, which give you opportunities to fully align with integrity, to choose integrity, and to honor your truth. Otherwise, this code would not anchor in. To choose blame or shame when these experiences present themselves is to deny your process of ascension. It would be out of alignment with your highest truth, which is love. Forgiveness is love, as you will come to understand more and more. Integrity effortlessly follows when you are conscious, when you are mindful, when you are aware of the intention, in terms of frequency, of your thoughts, actions, words, and choices, and choose accordingly. It is this mindfulness that allows you to stay in integrity. *Is this action, choice, or thought in alignment with the truth of who I am, as an extension of divine love? Or is it in alignment with another's viewpoint, another's frequency, or something else in the field? Is it really me?* These are questions for your exploration.

To anchor into integrity, you must know yourself very well. You must be fully connected to yourself as divine love. Your relationship with yourself is the most intimate of all. Do you treat it as such? It is in this relationship that the true depth of expansion happens. Many of you look to others, specifically a singular divine life partner, to unlock the depth of love within you. This is confusion. While this can be a helpful trigger for many of you, as you are on the path of ascension, you will integrate these energies within yourself. You realize that you are the world. You are full, whole, and divine, and you love yourself. Others might add more sweetness, perhaps more texture, but they are not your source of your sense of self. You are the one who holds the key to living fully embodied with the knowing of who you are.

If this is your most intimate relationship, the one with yourself, the one with yourself as the divine essence, there is a richness in your inner world that then translates to your outer world. This is what enhances your magnetism. This is how you receive more divine wisdom, because it is all with you. Where are you looking for it from outside yourself? It is all within you. Taking time to nurture this intimate relationship within yourself will catapult your ascension process. Many of you understand that when you are in a divine partnership, you will spend more time, attention, and energy on that relationship—on that person. Is this not what you also must offer for yourself? When you treat the relationship with yourself with as much importance as that with your divine life partner, you will unlock your next ascension codes. It is only through this process that you will develop an unwavering sense of integrity. How are you to choose what is in alignment for you and what is not if you are not deeply in the knowing of what is you to begin with? Integrity is honoring yourself. Integrity is honoring your authenticity. It is honoring truth. It is honoring love. It is honor. It is to live with the utmost respect for the divine in all. It is to live with humility.

What does it truly mean to live with humility? Feel into the truest frequency of the word. Allow yourself to live in the energy of being the student, allow yourself to teach you as much as you have to offer, allow the world around you to teach you everything it has to offer, allowing yourself to continue to expand, to be all aspects of yourself, and to explore infinite possibilities. To be in curiosity. To be open to learning and receiving and experiencing new things. To release any judgment about what is better than. To release comparison. To honor and respect others. To allow all around you to be your teachers. This is how you enter mastery. This is how you walk the path of ascension. If you already knew it, would you not already be living it?

See the beauty in all around you, and allow yourself to receive from it. Learn from it. When you believe you are better than others, you are not in humility. Realize the duality—again, raising your level of consciousness, choosing ascension. This is a different way of thinking. It feeds your ego to stay caught in duality—to stay caught in comparison. If you wish to stay in ego, it will be as you wish, but that is not the path to embodying your truth. It is time to move beyond this and access your highest potential and timelines, if you so wish. But this requires humility. It requires humility to see truth and to know truth. Otherwise, you would not look. Where you do not look, you cannot see. Where you do not look, you cannot find the gifts that are hidden. Humility allows you to look. Humility allows you to truly see. Humility allows you to drop the guard you have up that blocks more lessons, more gifts, and more love. Release the resistance and allow yourself to flow in consistent expansion. It drains your energy to fight the flow of humility. It is exhausting to pretend. It is exhausting to be out of alignment. It is exhausting to be out of integrity.

Humility is not dulling yourself down. Humility and confidence go hand in hand. When you are truly confident, humility is a byproduct. When you are truly confident, you need not prove yourself. You need not compare. You are open to learning, to growing, and to accessing all of the information around you through new experiences, new people, and new situations. You are open to seeing more—to exploring your past and using these lessons to shift your now, and to shift what you perceive to be the future. When you are truly confident, your ego is not attached to being right. This is true confidence. It is key to not confuse confidence with arrogance. Many believe confidence to be arrogance, and arrogance to be the opposite of humility, when in fact confidence is humility, and confidence is the opposite of cockiness. To be confident is an energy that radiates out from within you—a beautiful glow, an energy that others feel. True confidence is felt within you and by those around you. It need not be proven. Honor your beauty! Honor your gifts! Be proud of who you are! Celebrate this! Do the same for others.

As you release the duality, as you peel back the layers of the illusion of separation, you will see that celebrating yourself is celebrating all others, and celebrating others is celebrating yourself, because you understand that all are contributions to the larger essence, all are experiencing bits to add to the collective consciousness that contributes to the whole, the same way all members of the relay team are needed to finish the race, the same way five students break apart certain topics for their group project to put the entire project together as a whole, rather than trying to complete all portions individually. This is how the collective consciousness receives clearer, upgraded knowledge—when each individual, as you perceive them to be, fully embraces their experiences and opportunities for learning what is unique to them. It is honoring and celebrating this uniqueness, being grateful for it and for yourself, and seeing this in all others. See the beauty in all.

The code of humility allows you to receive. It allows you to explore. It allows you to remove anything that might have been blinding you before. Ego will blind you. Wanting to be correct, wanting to prove yourself, and committing to blissful ignorance will blind you. You are craving something deeper. In order to ascend, you must fully receive the experiences and lessons for your soul's highest evolution. It requires humility to reflect on what energies within you are ready to be transmuted and where you can love more, forgive more, and embody more of your truth. This is what humility allows—clarity, openness, and change.

If you are not already ascended, then of course change will be required for expansion. This is what it is to shift your vibration and to unlock more gifts—it is all change. The change is beautiful! It is in alignment with the natural flow of things! Where you are not in alignment with humility is where you directly block your path of ascension, for it requires commitment to evolution. It requires reflection, awareness, and seeing clearly. This is commitment to truth. You are not committed to truth if you are choosing to stay blind. Where you are not aligned with humility is where you are staying in darkness. Who does this really serve? It is up to you to align with your process of ascension. It is up to you to align with truth.

Be confident. This allows for humility. This allows surrender. It creates deep safety within your system overall when you feel safe to be humble, and when you are ready to look at all aspects of yourself lovingly. When you are open to your paradigm shifting, when you are open to changing the way you have done things before, when you are open to optimizing your processes, and when you are open to exploring the unknown—this is living with humility. This is one of the most honorable codes of all.

Again, humility is not doubting yourself. It is not dulling yourself down or hiding yourself. It is allowing your light to fully shine. It is fully embodying authenticity. It is being so confident that you are truly ready to be the student. Where you have decided that you already know it or that you've already done it is where you rob yourself of the opportunity to deepen your knowledge, to broaden your perspective, to ingrain the truth into your field, or to shift it. There is no downside to being in humility. It is openness. It is receiving. It is a requirement to allow your fullest expression of self if you desire to be in true humility—to anchor in this frequency. Allowing others to see your truth is humility. Coming forward as your purest, most open-hearted, most authentic self— this is confidence, and this is humility. Surrender to your authenticity. Surrender to your truth. This is honor. This is integrity. This is humility.

Do not be afraid to shift your ways. Do not be afraid to forgive yourself or another. Do not be afraid to apologize—this is one of the most respectful, integrous acts of all. It requires true confidence and true love. Do not be afraid to open your eyes to a new truth. Do not be afraid to learn from another. Do not be afraid to allow yourself to learn from all around you—this is the point! This is what it is to be on the path of ascension. It is a commitment to receiving more, unlocking more, and embodying more. This is accessed through deepening your relationship with yourself, but also through fully receiving what is available from all around you, as the divine works through all. There is no need to judge how the wisdom comes through or whom it comes through. It is an exciting thing that it *is* coming through, and it is so valuable! A constant elaboration on the lesson! It is through allowing yourself to be the student that you open yourself up to this process. When you are in full integrity, you are in humility. You are in true confidence. You are forever the student, and in doing so you become the master. Your humility is the code that allows you to receive the process, to receive the shift, and to receive the transformation.

TABLET IV:
TRUST

To live with higher wisdom is to trust the divinity within you, and to fully trust yourself. It is aligning with full trust that allows you to follow the ascension journey and access more of what is available to you. This code is to live from trust in your soul instead of from the fear of the ego.

Here we come to the Tablet of Trust—the key to allowing yourself to fully receive your truth and honor your truth. If you do not trust, you will not take action in alignment with the truth that you know. This is to trust yourself. So often you spend your lives looking for a reason why, looking for evidence, looking for proof, trying to rationalize what cannot be rationalized. This is because you have fallen out of trust with yourself. Look to yourself lovingly, and remember that you can trust yourself. How would it feel to live in a house with someone your whole life and know that they do not trust you? It would not feel very well in your system. You would feel the dissonance in the home and the discomfort in relating. There might be a piece of you that feels hurt, or resentful, or wondering why after all these years trust still wasn't built. And so it is with you, within you—between you, your vessel, your intuition, your mind, your body, and your soul—the different aspects of you that are all of you. This is where we find misalignment, this is where we find dissonance in the system, this is where things fall out of balance—when you don't trust.

To fully trust is to set yourself free. It is to free yourself from the chains that keep you caught in the system of other people's rules, perceptions, and lies. It is to free yourself. When you trust yourself, who can control you? This allows you to take responsibility for yourself! This allows you to see beyond the game. This is to take full control over your reality. To do so requires trust within yourself. Where do you not acknowledge your own truth? Where do you not trust it? Where do you look for external validation or evidence that it is okay for you to follow your truth and live your truth?

You can only build trust if you start leaning into it, and you will see again and again that you do know. That you can trust. That it is not a trick. That the divine is always supporting you. That the divine moves through you. That you embody divine wisdom that others might not understand, but they do not need to understand it. That you embody divine wisdom that is simply known—it is not something you must read in a book, and it is not something that needs external research to be proven! Isn't it curious how so many cling to research needing to be done to feel as though they know? This is quite literally pulling apart the trust within themselves—out-sourcing it when it is meant to be in-sourced. It's an inner process—when it is known, when it is felt. The truest thing you can know is your own wisdom. This is what is real for you, and you feel this in your body. And so, do you trust yourself? If you had full trust in yourself, what decisions would you make?

When you ask questions related to how to discern or how to know, this is pointing to where you do not trust yourself. This is your opportunity to become more precise with your questions. Often your questions are, in themselves, the answers you seek. What would it look like for you to trust yourself over anyone else? This is resilience. This is honor. This is knowing yourself. This is comfort with your own truth and living it out. When you are not living your truth, when you do not know your truth, when you avoid truth, it will be difficult to trust yourself. But when you are firm and resolute in your knowing, when you are clear on the frequency—trust is natural. The only way through is to trust. What feels like trust from an energy of hoping something will work out moves into the truest version of trust—a knowing. One could trust but have doubt underneath, and then take the leap, or one can trust with the knowing that they will be held on the other side.

When did this trust fall apart? What experiences influenced you to believe you could not trust yourself? Here you might find deep pockets of emotion that must be looked at—the deep pockets of emotion house experiences where you lost faith. Experiences where you could not understand why something happened or how it could have happened. Experiences where what you trusted in let you down. But tuning into these pockets of emotion is how you find the lessons. It is where you can find different perspective. Things are not always as they seem in the moments when you experience them, and when you are committed to your ascension, you will see things from a new perspective. Where you are still holding onto pockets of emotion from times when you felt hurt, betrayed, disappointed, or let down is where you block your own trust. You must face your questions and doubt head-on if you wish to seed them with light and understand them for what they really are, rather than the illusion. A common practice for many is to judge an experience later on, make meaning out of it, then put it in a box never to be explored again, and then live by that story. This is how you stay in illusions. This is how you stay in immaturity. This is how you block yourself from broader perspectives and uncovering the nuances of situations. The moments when you feel intense emotions are the most important in your process of soul evolution, growth, transformation, learning, completing contracts, and adding to the collective knowledge. You must look in these places if you wish to develop trust.

If you do not trust yourself, you will not move forward in alignment with your truth, and that is your block to being truth, which is your highest code of ascension. Where have you lost trust in the creator? In the divine? In love itself? These are the real places to explore. These are the real questions to ask. When did that begin? Why was it perceived as such? Why is it easier to blame the divine, to blame love, to decide that you do not trust love, that you do not believe in love, than it is to see where the ego is trapped in a story? Why jump to blaming all there truly is—love? This is the collective block. This is where the energy has been stuck for quite some time, as people started to make meaning of their experiences by deciding that all there truly is—love—was to blame, and therefore could not be real. This is a misunderstanding of love. This is a misunderstanding of divinity. This is labeling from a human perspective. This is feeding into low-frequency programs that encourage you to put your trust into people and beliefs that are not living truth. This is how you got there.

To experience difficult circumstances is not necessarily indicative of the absence of love. Where has love been the scapegoat? This is when you decided not to trust—when you made love the scapegoat. It is similar to how you might blame a loved one for something and fuel an argument with them rather than who the conflict is really with, when perhaps it was that loved one who has held you through the pain and the sadness the whole way through. And so, why blame them? You know, deep down, love will heal. There is confusion between mind and intuition. Your intuition knows to redirect you to love itself, but your brain thinks it is the "issue," when in fact that which aligns you with your path of healing, love, is there to protect you. It is always there to hold you. In moments when you lose trust in the divine, lose trust in love, what would it feel like for you to turn directly to it? Instead of deciding it does not exist simply because you felt something you perceived to be something else in the moment, what if you turned to it, called to it, and asked it to hold you? Asked it to make itself known? Love has never forgotten you. It is always with you.

When you start to ask for what you need, when you start to give love and the divine essence of all the opportunity to show up for you, when you are open to knowing it is always with you, always there for you—this is how you trust again. You might have experienced a loved one leaving or changing their mind, and you felt the abandonment. You felt the conditions of their love. Love itself, divine love, is unconditional. It does not leave, abandon, or reject. It is always there to hold you, to heal you, and to support you. Always. Can you trust this? And if not, ask yourself why? Who is that from? Is that the belief you wish to live with? If you are committed to that belief, then you are not committed to your path of truth. It is up to you. It might feel easier in the moment to stay in the stories of a child, looking to blame or judge, but it is certainly much harder for you to live that way in the grand scheme of things. In the overall vision of your life path, love is the path of flow. Truth is the path of least resistance, when you look from a bird's eye view.

You must trust your truth. You must trust your inner knowing. You must trust love. When you fully trust love, you always choose in alignment with it. When you trust truth, you listen to it, and you make decisions in accordance with it. When you are too afraid to follow your heart, when you are too afraid to live your truth, you are not in trust. If you will not trust, then how can you receive something greater? To trust is a choice. You can decide to trust. Tune into yourself, into your soul knowing, and you will be guided to what you can trust. Knowing the vibration of what deserves your trust will allow for clarity. Not everyone deserves your trust, for your trust is a gift. You trust is pure love. It is a treasure, a true gift.

In commitment to your truth, in commitment to seeing beyond the illusions, you must look at what is in your reality and what is in alignment with love. Who in your field is showing you, through how they live, how they love, and how they show up, that they are truly deserving of your trust? Many of you have lost trust because you have put your trust in those who are not in alignment with their truth, those who are not living from the love that is within them. You pay the price when you decide that another's commitment to illusions and ego will prevent you from trusting at all from then on. To trust itself is not to be tossed aside. The key is to be more discerning with whom you trust.

When you are aligned with your internal guidance system, when you know the voice of your soul, when you know the frequency of love, when you know the frequency of truth, you can discern who is ready to be trusted and who is not. Just because your soul is telling you not to fully trust another does not make them "bad" or "wrong"—notice where the ego likes to create stories to justify nonresonance. The ego likes to explain what doesn't need to be explained. There can be many reasons why you are not guided to trust someone or something. Perhaps you are being pulled toward a more aligned relationship, perhaps that person must go down another path to learn their own lessons, or perhaps the timing is off.

Listen to your soul. Listen to the resonance. Look at how people are truly showing up for you and for themselves. Where are you justifying the actions of others and then allowing this to limit your trust? You will feel a sense of safety and calm around those you can trust. You will know. There might be people in your life who are lovely, who have beautiful hearts, but this does not necessarily mean that you are to put your trust in them, that you are to share this gift. Discern. If there are people in your field you know you cannot trust in general, then this is a place to look. This is where your energetic availability for higher frequency relationships becomes blocked.

What would it feel like to be able to fully trust everyone in your life? To feel their love and support? To exchange unconditional love? To know forgiveness is always available to you? To release the weight off your shoulders and let yourself show the truest, most authentic version of yourself? This is what is possible when you surround yourself with those you can trust.

What of trusting the divine? What of trusting the path, the process? You must understand what beliefs and what stories you have created about how the world works. Is it all against you? Is it all working against you to bring you down? Or is it all for you? Is it all uplifting you? If the essence of Source is love, then love is threaded within everything. To imagine a world created where everything is against you is to stay in the illusion that fear, hate, and greed are the source of all, which you will see again and again is not true. Choose light and you will see it for yourself. You will live the experience. The light drowns out the darkness—this is known to you. Put darkness and light in one room, and all you will see is light.

When you tune into your inner truths and start to recognize areas where you can take leaps of faith, why is it that you don't believe you will be held? Why do you believe you will fall? This is where you do not trust yourself. This is where you do not trust the divine. This is where you believe that what is within you cannot be trusted, and that does not feel good at all! Reflect on times when you have followed your intuition, your knowing, and your truth. Perhaps in the moment you felt discomfort. The question is—was it really your discomfort, or was it that of people around you? Was it the discomfort of your soul or your ego? And how did it turn out? It was expanding you. It was recalibrating you. It was aligning you with joy every time. It was putting you back on the path of joy. When you have spoken your truth, when you have trusted your inner knowing, you have realigned with love each time. It has always led you to expansion and growth.

How has it felt to follow your truth? When you have trusted what you need to do, what you need to say, what you need to explore, this is where you are being guided to your gifts and lessons. Many of you hesitate to trust your intuition, to trust the signs, to trust the divine support that comes in your field. It is as real as anything else. In fact, it is the purest form of a sign. If you ask a friend for advice, and you ask for a sign from the divine source of love, which will be influenced by someone's ego? Which has its own projections? Divine love is truth. There is no dulling it down. It will tell you exactly how it is. It will tell you exactly what you need to hear. It is in interpretation where the ego might get in the way, but when aligned with truth, humility, and integrity, you can trust your process of discernment.

You will not feel confident in your process of discernment if there is a deep piece of you that knows your ego or mind tends to get in the way. How would it feel to fully surrender to yourself? This is what it looks like to trust. This is what it looks like to flow. It is trust that opens your field to greater experiences, to greater knowledge, and to deeper meaning. It is an opening energy. It is a collaborative energy. It is an energy of receiving. It is dropping resistance. When you find the flow of life, you feel good! When you trust, now energy can move and shift. Now things that were not available to you before can drop in.

As you commit to ascension, as you commit to truth, as you commit to higher learning, paradigms will be shattered. That which you previously thought to be impossible, you will know to be possible. The gifts you didn't believe could be real—you will see them as your own as they come to light. But if you do not trust, you will not be able to see these things. You will not be open to receiving them. It could be right in front of your eyes, and you would turn your nose to it! Because you wouldn't trust.

This is how children are able to easily align with the energy of miracles—they trust. They allow themselves to create, to play, to explore, and to be curious. They do not have walls of ego around them, the walls of the mind that box them in, keeping them in one way of thinking, in one narrow view of reality. They are open. They are trusting. They trust when they are hungry, when they want to play, how they want to play, how they want to express themselves, what colors they want to use, and how they want to dress. They do not question themselves. They follow their joy! If you cannot trust your joy, what can you really trust? It is when your ego boxes you in, when your mind gets so loud, that you do not trust because trust is in alignment with soul. Trust is calm, nurturing, and loving. It allows you to be held.

If you have blocks to receiving love and to being held, you have a block with trust. How can you learn further, open further, and receive further if you do not trust? Trust wants to support you. This is where you can peel apart the definition of trust. What if trust was confidence? What if trust was knowing that the divine guidance that moves through you and around you is firm, is confident, is knowing, and is just as real as anything else? In fact, it is in alignment with love, and thus the truest frequency of truth, so why would it not be trusted? Notice how it feels for you to affirm—*I trust. I trust. I trust.* Feel that sense of relief!

There will be moments along the way when you will be asked to choose between your truth and someone else's. Your mind and your soul. This is where trust comes into play. The truth is that you are always trusting something or someone, so who is it? Are you trusting your soul or your ego? Your intuition or your mind? Yourself or your friends? The divine or the media? Those of you who struggle to trust and who ask how to trust, you are already trusting. Are you aware of who or what it is you are trusting? Again, this comes from a loving place of recognizing truth, of recognizing how you are showing up, of recognizing what you are aligning with, and of taking responsibility for your field. It all builds on each other.

To trust is to understand that when you set your intention, the divine moves through you and others to recalibrate your reality to this intention. It is always working for you. There are no coincidences. You will draw in teachers for your ascension in the way of people, information, and experiences, and then you must tune inward to crack open the kernels of knowledge. To trust is to recognize that it is always working when you are clear with your intention and energy. That is all it takes. To trust is to understand that what comes into your reality, the desires that rise within you, what comes up for you uniquely is all relevant and is all important.

Everything is significant, and that knowing is the exact tool you need for your next level of ascension, to unlock more truth, to unravel more layers, giving you access to exactly what you seek. It is giving you access to exactly what you need in that moment. If it is needed in that moment, it is available to you. This is different from wanting it, coming from the perspective of your ego. To trust is to remember the essence of divine love. It is to remember your divinity—to know this deep within you, and then you realize that from your call, from your intentions, from your clarity, what comes from within you in its purest essence is to be trusted, so you can trust those desires. To understand that when the book, or line, or person shows up in your field, that was from your intention, that was an answer to your call. It is always working. It is always being revealed to you.

That which you seek on a soul level is seeking you, but you must trust this. If you do not trust, then when it comes into your field, you will not notice it. You will overlook it or take it for granted. Be conscious and mindful. Do not overlook any single moment. One word can be that significant. As you drop into the wisdom of your body, into the wisdom of your soul, you can taste the richness of every moment, and suddenly, instead of feeling like life is passing you by, you realize that so much is available to you in every moment. Instead of waiting around, you are in the knowing that what is right now—whatever is right now—is exactly what is needed, whether that is quiet, silence, passion, awareness, a single thought, a noise, a reflection, or an observation. There is richness in the now. When you desire something and already think it is not here now, you are out of trust. Trust yourself. Trust your intention and your inner wisdom. Trust the divinity that flows through you.

With this is trusting your gifts and your desires. You were perfectly designed for this. You were perfectly designed with your unique genetic code and your unique soul code to be the fullest expression of love in your own way, to unlock what is meant to be unlocked, perfectly set up to be aligned with your ascension, with joy, with love, with all that you've ever desired on a soul level. This is not a coincidence. Where are you turning away from yourself? Where are you judging yourself? Where are you judging your goals and dreams? Where are you telling yourself that you cannot have what you desire—the divine desire that is the divine within you? Where do you reject your own divine essence? Your own truth? This is rejection of self. Send it love! See it with love, the same way you would talk to a child. The world is their oyster.

Where have you turned your back on your gifts? Where have you turned your back on that which is natural for you? Perhaps ask those you love what they see your gifts to be—this can give you some perspective. Reflect on what is easy for you and natural for you. What did you enjoy as a child? What would feel like play? This is all guiding you to your highest frequency. When you spend more time here, more of this frequency comes to you. Release the need for it to make logical sense—that is not the way of ascension. It if were, you would already be there. It is not the way of truth. Truth is a knowing. It is not the way of higher levels of consciousness, it is not the way of the quantum for things to make linear sense. You can choose to drive the car or fly the plane, but trying to do both at the same time will get you nowhere.

Trust that what is within you is for you. Trust that what brings you joy is your guiding light—why would it be any other way? Trust your design—who you really are. This is how you find flow. You are meant to be in this ease and grace. In following this path you are able to reach mastery, because you are following what is natural for you. Your natural gifts, your natural joy—this is within you for a reason, as your signpost of where to "start." As you follow it, you deepen your mastery or skills, or you can spend your whole life trying to be someone you are not. This is resistance. It does not feel good for you to spend so much time trying to master something you aren't here to master.

You are aware of what it feels like to meet someone who is fully in their flow, in their mission, in their purpose. You perceive the ease. That ease is within you! The key is to listen to it and not judge it. Why judge your joy? If your joy was a person, how would that judgment feel to it? Would you judge the joy of a friend, a lover, or a child? You would celebrate it! As you learn to celebrate the joy, you open yourself up to your greatness. When you turn your back on your gifts, when you turn your back on your natural joy, you turn your back on your greatness. This is how you block yourself from stepping into your greatness, and this is what you are here to do. To shine brightly. To be seen clearly! Stop dulling yourself.

Trusting your joy and your gifts is in alignment with your truth. It is in alignment with your confidence, your humility, and your responsibility. If you have a natural gift, a desire within you, a gift within you, it was placed within you. You were designed this way. It is your responsibility to go deeper into it, to explore it more deeply, to deepen your mastery, to share this with others who do not have the same gift or the same joy. Where you dull your light, where you do not live your truth, where you do not deepen your mastery of your natural gifts, is where you are out of alignment with both truth and responsibility—responsibility to yourself, to the collective, to the divine, to your essence as the divine, and to ascension.

Your gift might be a tangible skill. It might be an energy. Your natural gift is in fact being the most authentic version of you. Some might find their mastery in a craft, but many will find their mastery in the way in which they show up, in the way in which they live, in their ability to be their most authentic selves. What are you most drawn to? What is flow for you? How do you enjoy moving through the world? How do you enjoy spending your time? What do you enjoy learning about or pondering? What do you enjoy looking at? What do you enjoy feeling? Allow yourself to flow to it.

Your mastery desires to come through—you need only make space for it. It is not hidden deep within you. It is the most natural, obvious thing. It is the thing you've loved all along. It is doing it in the way that feels like flow to you. It is effortless. It is flow. It is the divine flowing through you. When you follow this path, mastery is readily available to you. When you are out of alignment with your gift, the mastery will feel like an exhausting struggle. This is your sign that it is not in alignment the way it currently is, and something greater is available for you. What is for you uniquely allows you to activate your full magic and power, to anchor in your ascension process. It is not better or worse than another. It is what is uniquely aligned for you. It is always revealing itself in your field. It is always trying to find you. It is always trying to make itself known to you. It has been right in front of you all along! There is no need to make it more difficult on yourself. Trust what wants to move to you and through you, and see it from a place of love.

Here you trust. Here you remember. You return back to the wisdom within you, to your unique way of moving through the world and being in the world. You come home when you trust. You release the weight, the shield, the armor, and the blocks to receiving love. You discern. You require that those in your field match you, expand you, and open you to more that is in alignment with truth. That those around you live their truth. You sink into being truth. You surrender to truth. You surrender to your Highest Self—your highest alignment. You surrender to love. This is trust.

TABLET V: SURRENDER

Upholding the codes of truth is to surrender the ego, is to surrender any false sense of control, is to surrender to what is the highest truth. You must release attachment to any previous identity, way of being, way of thinking, or anything external if you are committed to the highest truth.

Surrender to love. Surrender to the process. Many expect ascension to be a step-by-step, linear, practical process. In some ways it is, and in others it is not. Your ego likes a step-by-step process so you know what's coming, so you can get ahead and do it on your own timing. This is where you are not surrendering to the divine energies that move through you. This is where you do not trust that all is happening exactly as it should, right on time. Ascension is first and foremost an energetic process. You want the practical to unlock the energetic, but it is the energetic that unlocks the physical process. It is the energetic shift, the unlocking of these frequencies within you, the full activation of and the embodiment of these energies that then effortlessly unlock the physical. The steps that are practical and tangible fall into place easily. That is the simple part—that is the part behind the door—but first you have to find the key, and then use the key to open the door. It is not the other way around.

If you are looking for a step-by-step guide to ascension, it is already within you. It is already known to you. All you must do is peel back the layers of the ego that are blocking you from seeing it, that are blocking you from knowing it. All you have to do is embody the codes that are being activated through these tablets within you and live from these energies. All else will follow. The steps will be laid out before you. Again, this is the easy part. Following the practical steps—the "to-dos" without the energetic shifts—without unlocking the codes does nothing at all. You must set the stage energetically for ascension to happen, for it to activate—otherwise nothing will happen. Otherwise it will feel like resistance. Your ego might want the practical steps. It wants to be told what to do to get there, but why does it want this? Because you want to control it. Because you are not in alignment with surrender. Can you surrender to the process? Can you surrender to the flow of things? Can you surrender to your soul? To the divine moving through you?

To surrender is to allow your mind and ego to drop their defenses—to drop their blocks to you living your truth. This is surrendering to truth. Surrendering to *your* truth. When you fight your truth, you feel the discomfort, you feel the resistance, you feel that everything in your life starts to feel stuck, because you are not in alignment with your ease. Your truth is your path! When you surrender to it, the knowing is clear. You know what to do. You know how to act. When you act in alignment with your truth, when you surrender to it, suddenly you realize so many emotions and thoughts you had kept beneath the surface that you weren't allowing yourself to know, feel, or see all along. You ask yourself, *How was I blind to this? How was I living like this?* You could not see it because you would not allow yourself to. In this example, you see how opening yourself up to truth and surrendering to it is how all that must be revealed for you to clear out lower frequencies, release the density, feel your feelings, and tap into your inner wisdom comes through. It all comes through when you surrender to truth, and it is from this place of surrender that living your truth does not feel difficult.

What would it look like for you to live from a place of surrender to the divine timing, to the divine flow, to the divine moving through you, surrendering to the higher aspects of you taking you to whatever you're meant to be doing, surrendering to your soul desires? This is trust. This is love for yourself. This is love—not forcing yourself to be someone you're not, not forcing yourself or others to be on the timeline of your ego, which is a made-up timeline based on…what? A sense of urgency that is not truly real. There is nowhere to get to. It is all now. It is an illusion that what you seek is not readily in your now. From that illusion, you keep yourself stuck, you keep yourself in unhappiness and discomfort, and then what comes into your field?

When you commit to ascension, and when you commit to truth, you will be pushed to surrender. This is love. From surrender comes your knowing, your effortless flow, and your alignment. When you have committed to ascension and to truth, notice where you feel pushed, brought to your knees. Where your ego has been in the way will be shown to you, ready to be seen. Are you willing to see it for yourself? You will be pushed to surrender to your truth. You will be pushed to surrender to where you have been living in illusion. You will be pushed to surrender so you can release the resistance, so you can release the density, so you can release the lower frequencies. This is from love! This is surrendering to love. This is allowing yourself to be who you were meant to be.

Where are you being pushed to surrender, and what is there for you? Why do you hold on so tightly when it is not the natural flow of things to stay stuck? You are fighting what is for you, rather than sinking into the flow of your ultimate evolution and highest lessons. This is how life moves more quickly in the ways you wish it to—when you follow the flow of energy and where it naturally moves, allow yourself to be in joy and curiosity of where you are taken, and surrender to each moment. Allow yourself to surrender to each moment. Surrender to your emotions, so they do not get stuck. Surrender to what is underneath the emotions. This is where you find the awareness of your thoughts, your passions, your desires, your beliefs, your intentions, and your energy.

Surrender to the moment. This is where you surrender to beauty and allow yourself to receive it. It invites you to fully receive. The divine wants you to receive! Your highest self wants to receive! You are worthy of receiving. You are meant to receive. You are not meant to grasp for things the whole way through. It is the difference between doggy-paddling for hours in the ocean and simply floating on your back as you look up at the beautiful sky. You can choose. If you are in the experience, why not surrender to it? When you are in trust, you recognize what is coming up in your reality is a new lesson or piece of wisdom for you, whether this is a situational experience or a thought. Surrender to it so you can go into it. It is only through going into it that you unlock it, and then you find the gold within. That is required for your next step. One at a time.

If you resist, if you look elsewhere, if you live in the distractions, it will come back your way. It will continue to come back your way, whether in the same form or a different one, until you surrender to it and get in the middle of it. Many of you avoid this because you do not want to feel the feelings, and this is where you are afraid of your own wisdom. This is where you are afraid of your truth. The truth is within your emotions. It is within experiencing them fully. It is on the other side of them that the clarity comes through. It is your body's divine wisdom. When you resist your emotions, you keep them stuck. Allow the energy to flow through. Surrender to your path, and you will find joy. Surrender to your joy, and you will find mastery. Surrender your ego, and you will live as your purest expression. You will live from soul. Surrender to love, and you will know what to do. It will be effortless to live as love when you surrender to it. It will be effortless to forgive, and from this you find freedom. To live in surrender will allow you to unlock the wisdom that you seek. You are here because you crave more. You crave truth.

The ascension process is energetic. It is emotional. It is physical. You will be brought to surrender each step of the way so that wherever your identity is attached to any single thing, wherever your ego is attached to any single thing, wherever you are in an addiction or 3D anchor, it will be made known to you. This is where you can release the density. You cannot release the density if you do not surrender to the process. Surrender to the process itself and how it wants to flow. Surrender to the stages, and to the path. Some might find it to be more emotional than physical, others more physical than emotional, and some might find it is more about unraveling their beliefs. The exact process will be different for all because your surrender guides you. Your surrender guides you to where you are still in attachment and density, and how this shows up will be different for each of you. This brings you to the lessons that allow you to fully unlock your unique energetic codes, and thus your full power.

Surrendering to the process allows you to step into mastery with your gifts. When you release resistance and live in surrender, your spiritual abilities and mastery will unravel effortlessly in whatever way is fully aligned with your highest expression. Release judgment about how this should look. Where you are still in judgment is where you are not in surrender, and this is how you slow down the process. Many of you try to control things, thinking it will speed up the process when, in fact, it does the opposite. Surrender allows you to flow places you would not expect, in ways you wouldn't have planned for yourself from the place of the mind. Surrender is the shortcut. It is the fastest way there. When you surrender, you will sink into the flow of ascension and get there much more quickly.

And so, you must surrender to the process and how it plays out. You must also surrender to what it means. Where do you like the idea of ascension, of mastery, of truth, but not what is required to get there? Where do you tell yourself you are ready to live as truth, yet only if it means you stay comfortable? This is not truth. This is ego. The process is inherently a process of surrender to a new way of being. Where your ego only wants to go a certain way, you are still attached. You must detach from your ego's pull. Release attachment to any single belief about what it will be, what it will look like, and how you will get there. It will look different for all.

Where you are attached is where you add resistance. You are thinking too hard! When you are in surrender, you need not think much about it at all. You simply observe and allow. Allow life to flow through you. Allow the divine to flow through you. Allow life to flow to you. Allow the divine to flow to you. Allow what is meant for you to flow to you. But it cannot flow to you if you are controlling the doors you open. Listen. Follow the signs. When you trust in love and when you trust in truth, surrender is natural. To live in truth—to live in humility and integrity—is to live in surrender. Surrender to "needing" anything, and be open to receiving. To live in truth, humility, and integrity is to surrender to where you can learn, expand, and grow. This is how you ascend. This is how you shift and change. Where you are attached to being right or already knowing the way is not surrender, it is resistance. It is choosing to keep the energy stuck.

When you are in surrender, you allow the truth to be made known to you, which will either serve as confirmation or as a place for you to evolve your wisdom, which is what you truly seek. Take a deep breath. Surrender. Listen to what you need. You know. Listen to what you desire deep within, from a place of love, the voice of your soul. Surrender to your joy. Allow yourself to pause and feel. Surrender to your truth—it is your guiding light. It is your ascension. It is the string that carries you to each exact step of the process and allows it to unfold in the fastest, most aligned way for you. Truth is your guiding light, but you must be in surrender to allow it to guide you. Will you surrender to the divine carrying you, holding you, and guiding you? To surrender is to allow it all to fall back into alignment. You must release the resistance for higher frequencies to carry you. You must release resistance to fully receive all of the love, support, and wisdom that is ready to pour into you, move through you, activate you, and hold you.

When you feel the energy is stuck, get curious about where you are being asked to surrender. You will know deep within. It is the place you are trying too hard. It is the place you are trying to force. It is the place that feels heavy and sticky. It is where you are trying to make it work. It is not in alignment with ease. It is most likely the place that has been on your mind, or what you have been intentionally pushing out of it. It is where you are in your own way. When you step out of your own way and surrender, you get in the middle of it, and the knowledge is there. The wisdom is there. The lesson is there. The insight is there. The new perspective, the new way of being or doing—it was right there all along! You just had to drop the resistance. You had to release trying to figure it out. Stop trying to find it. Let it reveal itself to you. Surrender to the emotion. Go underneath it. Allow it to not make sense so it can drop in. Underneath it, you might be pleasantly surprised. From there you unlock the code, you integrate the wisdom, and you move into a new energy. This moves the energy along once again, and you flow directly to your next step. To surrender allows you to get out of your own way. You are the only one who can block yourself! And when you live in surrender to the divine within, you experience ease.

Surrender is not giving up. It is not giving away your power—this is not surrender in alignment with the divine truth of who you are. Surrender is releasing your resistance to truth. It is allowing yourself to explore all options, to see the infinite possibilities, to release attachment so that what is beyond your conscious awareness of possibility can come through for you. You limit your options when you try to figure it out or make it happen. Surrender, and your ascension process will astound you with miracles and magic! You will feel the flow. You will feel love move you like the wind. You will feel the magic, live the magic, and see the magic. From there, more comes. Your body, your mind, and your heart are capable of far more than your current realm of beliefs allows, but you must be open to other possibilities in order to experience them.

All is possible. When you surrender, you unlock the quantum. You unlock your highest possibilities and your highest ascension because you release limitations. Resistance is how you limit yourself. And so, the code of surrender allows you to fully claim your inner power, to fully claim your gifts, to fully claim your wisdom—it has been right there all along! Right within you! Right in the middle of your experiences! Right underneath your emotions! Right in front of you!

When you are ready to claim your mastery, your spiritual maturity, and your innate wisdom, you surrender to energy beyond what is seen. You surrender to the knowing that what is in the dense form of this reality is only a fraction of what is available. You surrender to the infinite. You make yourself available for miracles and for knowledge that will shift your reality as you know it. This is how you make yourself available to receive. This is surrendering to your truth—the highest code, that which sets you free. Where is your truth speaking to you and tugging on you? Where is it asking you to surrender? Surrender what you think you know. Release what you are clinging to, and allow what is in highest alignment for where you are headed to come to you, based on vibrational resonance.

As you live the path of ascension, your frequency will continue to shift. It is holding onto what was resonant before that will keep you stuck and leave you feeling defeated, exhausted, and stagnant. You must live in surrender. Live in the release. Allow what is meant to come with you to come with you, but do not try to force it. This will only hold you back and rob others of the opportunity to shift and change as well. You will feel yourself outgrowing things consistently. Observe this as a sign of your field upgrading and recalibrating. This is part of the process. Everything is shifting. Will you allow it? Or will you get in the way?

Where your truth is asking you to surrender is where it is asking you to receive more love. It is asking you to sink into divine love. It is asking you to claim the purest form of love. Your surrender allows you to flow, and it allows you to receive. This is how you experience divine love in its purest form. The path is truth, and the way is surrender.

TABLET VI: LOVE AND FORGIVENESS

The commitment to truth is the commitment to love, and living from pure love is living with forgiveness. It is aligning with the pureness of love that allows you to see the truth easily and effortlessly and allows you to act in accordance with these higher truths. It is love that breaks you free from illusion.

Truth is a piercing frequency, and love softens its edges. In this tablet we will explore love and forgiveness, which are one and the same. You speak of love very often, and of forgiveness, but usually not in alignment with their divine definitions. And so, to fully receive this tablet, you must be in surrender and commit to the highest truth above all else. Otherwise you will not be able to see, to admit, or to acknowledge where you are not being love. It is in those places that you must patch up the holes and fill in the gaps, and this illuminates your entire experience. This brings more love to you. Open your heart to receive this tablet fully, and this is where you will expand. These codes are what make you you—living in love. Living from love. Living as love. When you are in conscious awareness, when you are mindful of how you move through the world and why you do what you do, why you say what you say, why you think what you think, and why you feel what you feel, you will come to the direct realization of where you are coming from love and where you are not.

The divine definition of love is unconditional. Where are you living in conditions? This is not to allow others to meet you with lower frequencies and walk all over you—it is to uphold the frequency of love in every interaction. Boundaries are love. You will start to unravel what you have been told is love—obligation, people-pleasing, dulling yourself down, not rocking the boat, and so on. Reflect on this—what is it to love? When have you truly felt love? What have you been taught is love? What are the conditions? You must first start with love for yourself, and this emanates out to others. When you treat yourself fully with love, you naturally move through the world in this way. Others will see your light and your love. It is a softening, healing, transmuting frequency.

When you meet a lower frequency with love, explore this from different angles. What is of the highest love for me? What is of the highest love that moves through me? When you are anchored into love, your perceptions will change. There is no more room to try to make another wrong or right or to categorize into good or bad when you are seeing through the lens of love. Where there is a wound, a hurt, or a pain, the only way through is to heal, with the frequency of divine love. To hold someone in love is healing, is expanding, is ascending. Can you hold yourself in this way first? Notice where you are living in obligations, in shoulds, in judgment, and in resentment. This is not love. Notice where you will not forgive. Where you will not forgive is where you hold onto frequencies that are not serving you or any others. They are feeding dis-ease in your system. This is where you are withholding love. Where are you withholding love for yourself or others?

Love is an unlimited resource. It is within everything. It is the highest power source of all. It is the clarity you seek. It is the aligned path. But this calls forward the acknowledgment of where you are addicted to pain or sadness. What is it you are truly seeking? You will get the highest of highs from pure divine love. Many think they do not because they have not received or felt divine love—now is your time to call it forward. Now is your time to release any ways you might be settling. It is your time to know what you are deserving of and what is available to you—divine love—as this runs through you, as this has created you, as it is within every cell of your being, as it is the energy that supports all. Where have you turned away from it?

Moment by moment, ask yourself if you are coming from the intention of love for yourself and others. These two do not oppose each other, but rather align quite beautifully when you zoom out for a moment, when you shift your perception out of ego and into the heart space. When you act from love for yourself, you do not hold onto low-frequency energies toward another. You do not shoot energy darts of lower vibrations to another. You forgive and send love. Perhaps this is setting boundaries, but also allowing your perceptions some space to recalibrate to the energy of love.

Many of you wish for people to change, and I will remind you that you cannot depend on this. You cannot expect it. It is their choice. But when you come from love, this gives other people the opportunity to change. Hold your frequency, and allow others to show you that they can shift and step into a different energy. Many only require the opportunity to start to shift. Many have not seen another way. When you release the old ways of being, what is expected, and what has been common, and you align with this new way of love, you set the tone of the new earth. You shift the possibilities. You create the possibilities. Moment to moment, those around you notice an opening in the field. It feels good to rise into love, to live from love, and to see an example of another way.

When you understand that much of human behavior has simply been copying what was modeled, has been reactive, has been from fear, you can perceive from compassion. It is from this place that you offer an opportunity for the vibration to shift. A new model. A new way. It is not your responsibility to push another to their change—that is their choice. But it is your responsibility, if you are to align with ascension, to uphold the codes of love and truth for yourself and those around you, as you all are one. It is your responsibility to keep your field aligned with love. Anywhere you recognize you are not, this is where you experience wisdom, this is where you receive higher knowledge, this is where you can create a new shift and recalibrate the field, and you have anchored in a new energy.

You can always shift the energy, but you must first acknowledge what is occurring and then choose differently. Holding the belief that it has to stay the way it has been is connected to where you will not forgive and where you choose to hold onto lower vibrations, which is self-punishment. This is not from love! Punishing yourself creates more dissonance in your system. How are you punishing yourself? You know the feeling of this. Where did you first learn this? The energy of punishment has been deeply embedded in the system for quite a long time, and this is one of the deep illusions that has been used to control people and hold them in lower states of consciousness, because they feel the fear.

What are you afraid of? When you understand the essence of all is love, and that love is the most powerful energy of transmutation, nothing can hold you back. But when people are kept in illusions of fear, and they believe that fear is more powerful, they will feed into these energies of punishment. Here you find there is another way. This is instant liberation. Choose love always. Love is divine protection. Love is divine healing. Even the lowest frequencies will melt, shift, and be transmuted when met with love. Why do you feel the pull to meet fear, greed, or anger with more of the same? This is a reaction from the ego, this is a wound of the child—this is not from a place of healing. This is not from the place of the soul. When you align with your soul, you will release self-punishment. Where have you used self-punishment to motivate yourself? Do you see how this is feeding into the system, the overall use of fear to control you? You must shift this within yourself if you desire the external reality to shift out of this pattern as well.

When you tune into the energies of love and forgiveness, you feel the light. You feel the softness. You feel the glow. You feel the safety. It can move you to tears. It is what you have been desiring all along because it is your truest essence. It is what you have been desiring all along because it is you. Because it is alignment. Because it is truth. Because it is your natural state. When you tune into the energies of greed, anger, punishment, and fear, you feel the heaviness. You feel the density. You feel the duality. You feel the limitation. You feel the shackles. You feel blocked off from the infinite. Love is infinite. Love is the quantum. Love is all. Fear is limitation. Release your limitations.

Start with yourself. Start with forgiveness. Start with acknowledging what you need to forgive yourself for. Acknowledge what you have not forgiven within yourself. Who have you not forgiven? Who are you still holding energy for? If you have not forgiven, you are still holding their energy in your field—that of the person or situation—and this is not serving you, as it keeps lower frequencies in your system, as it creates dis-ease, as it impacts the way you think in certain situations. When you clear out these low-frequency energies, you will think differently. You will perceive differently. You will feel different. Those low-frequency energies are your blocks to ascension. They are your blocks to truth, because you are putting on the glasses of fear, anger, or hurt, and so you see and perceive from this illusion. You must clear these energies to know truth, to live truth, to see truth, and to be truth. You must clear your vision.

Recognize what still needs to be forgiven, and allow yourself to explore why you have not. How does holding the grudge serve you? It does not allow for the highest wisdom or transformation of any involved. It keeps everyone stuck. Release the energy and send it lovingly back to the sender. Send it love. Send yourself love. Release the situation, for it was experienced at that time but there is no reason to keep living in it. There is no reason to keep holding it in your system. Allow it to float on, like a passing ship in the sea. This is how you stop living in timelines that do not serve you. Allow yourself to live in the present.

You cannot live in the present if you are living in the past or the future, but that is where many of you spend your time and energy. What is real now? What is available now? You will shift your energy and align with truth when you learn to be present right now and release everything else. Notice, observe, learn, integrate, and live in the now. When you fully live in the now, forgiveness is the only way, because you are not carrying what happened before into what is now, and everyone feels the opportunity to rise into the vibration of love. This is how you fully receive the highest form of love—you are present to now, experiencing the beauty of now, and experiencing the love available to you in this instant. Where you are living in the past is where you block your ability to receive.

This might upset some of you who misunderstand forgiveness as justifying what occurs or invalidating your feelings. They are not the same. Where you are triggered by the idea of forgiveness is where you are attaching illusory stories to what it means instead of being present in the now and allowing yourself an opportunity to fully embody love. No one else can block you from this—only you can. Where you do not want to forgive is where you are out of alignment with truth itself. This is one of the stickiest points for most of you, which is why it is so important. Living as love. Forgiving. The culture has become one of fear, holding grudges, and not allowing for forgiveness, which keeps people in fear. This does not feel good for any of you. It creates a system where you inherently block yourselves from ascension because you stay in self-punishment. When you recognize where you will not forgive, how would that feel for you on the receiving end? That does not feel like love.

Again, forgiveness does not mean invalidating your feelings or experience. It does not mean that you must take any specific action afterward. It does not mean you must ever engage with the person or experience again—maybe you will, and maybe you will not. The situations you must forgive are often also your greatest growth points. Some of these people might become your most powerful teachers. Your ego might not like your teachers, and that is okay. Allow yourself to be surprised.

Others might be released from your field. Forgiveness is just the release of any low-frequency energies that no longer serve you, and this allows you to see clearly. It allows you to stay in truth.

Why withhold forgiveness? Why hold the grudge? Why expect what happened before to happen again? Why project an old experience onto another person or situation, or even the same person or situation? This is where the fear, the anger, the resentment, and the grudges spiral in your system and keep you out of alignment with truth. They keep you in illusions and stories, rather than anchoring into the present and into love. When you do, truth is clear. The truth is clear of what has changed and what has not. The truth is clear of what might be available now that wasn't before. The truth becomes clear when you see from love.

This is a higher standard for yourself and others. You cannot control who rises to it. But this is shifting something that has been deeply embedded in your society for much time as a mechanism of control. If it feels like getting into a new groove, that's because it is. The old groove did not feel very good, and once you are living as love, you experience the ecstasy and freedom you have been seeking. You receive life. You receive infinite possibilities. You are able to see clearly and more broadly, you activate your full potential, you align with your gifts, and you deepen your experience. This is what it is to live from love. This shows up in sneaky ways. Where are you shaming or blaming another? Where are you abdicating responsibility? Where are you projecting or expecting? Where are you comparing? Where are you in the belief that you are not good enough? That another is not good enough? Where are you in the belief that there is not enough to go around?

Is this from love?

You will relate to people differently. You will uphold love and require this of those around you. If, in the now, others are not calibrated to this frequency, you will lovingly release them from your field, and if they choose to recalibrate, they will return again. And so, setting boundaries is love—this is love for yourself and your energy field. This is love for what is required of you to fully align with your mission and ascension. This is love for others, in calibrating your field to the frequency of divine love.

However, notice the energy of the boundaries themselves. Boundaries from certain frequencies might not come from love. Where are you setting boundaries from a place of fear? Of projection? Of anger? Of resentment? This is not a boundary of love. It is a barrier to protect the wound—a barrier that never allows it to heal. It might block its visibility, but it is still open. This wound must heal. You will become aware of where you are acting from your wounds.

When you ask yourself where the boundary is coming from— perhaps anger, fear, or sadness—you will start to uncover where you are hiding. Boundaries from love are different from those that are anchored into lower frequencies. Boundaries from love are not, in fact, about pushing people or things out. They are not a fence you put up around you. Boundaries from love are a recalibration of your standards and energy. They are you deciding what you would like to emanate out from your field, and therefore they are you deciding which frequencies will most easily find you. Everything else will not resonate and will be guided somewhere else. It is truly a refinement of your energetic field.

If your "boundaries" are a fence pushing people out, have you truly recalibrated your field? This is where your boundaries are actually fences—where you hide the wounds, where you are not taking responsibility for your own energy, where you are not clear in your truth, and where you are not living in love and forgiveness. It is where you are hiding. It is where you are abdicating responsibility for your healing, for your lessons, for your wisdom, for the codes of honor—upholding truth and integrity. Perhaps you choose a different word for boundaries when they are boundaries of integrity and love. It is not a boundary that is a fence, but shifting the frequency of your aura, and projecting out so much love that all that can meet it is more of the same.

You might ask, why is it so hard to forgive? Well, what are you used to? It is not hard to forgive, it is just out of alignment with your ego. It is related to the stories you hold about forgiveness and what that means—where you are projecting what it means. Forgiveness is not an excuse for another. Withholding forgiveness is where you continue to feed your ego, your fear, your duality, the illusion of separation, and the energy of comparison. It is where you are feeding into the energy of punishment, which affects you and those around you. Where are you sending out energies of punishment? It cannot come from you if it is not within you. What would it look like if you sent out the energy of love?

All you must do is decide—to align with love, to see as love, to be love, and to offer forgiveness. This is how you spread healing. It is not up to you whether or not others receive this, but it is up to you if you show up from a new level of consciousness and anchor fully into it. It is up to you if you release the baggage you are holding onto that is no longer serving you and is keeping you in a muddied, foggy perception of the world. How do you wish to see the world? It is lighter, it is fun, and it is joyful when you live as love and allow others to step into this. It feels wonderful to be met with love! It can transmute the lowest frequencies in an instant.

When you are crying, or when you are hurt, how does it feel when someone yells at you? And then, when you are crying, or when you are hurt, how does it feel when someone holds you with love and meets you with love? One is healing—it transmutes. The other feeds more low frequencies into the system. How do you want to be met? And what do you want to project out? This is what is in your field. You are responsible for your field if you are choosing ascension. You are responsible for your field if you are choosing truth. When you wonder why things are the way they are or why you feel the way you feel, look at your field. Look at how you are perceiving, what you are projecting out, what you are expecting, and how you are showing up. It is all in your vibration. The truth of what is isn't in the fear. It is not in the anger. It is not in the resentment. It is in love.

Forgiveness is how you release the anchors holding you back from your greatest shifts. As you forgive, you will feel an instant recalibration, you will feel an instant opening in your field to receive more love, you will feel your inner knowing and spiritual gifts turn on, and you will break free from the confines of time and space because you are no longer living in the past. You must embody forgiveness, feel forgiveness, and receive forgiveness to set yourself free from your current level of consciousness. Forgiveness opens the field for more love. Forgiveness is natural when you are living as love. What else can come from love? Love does not hold grudges. Love is truth.

In each moment, you can choose to live as love. What does that mean? Set the intention for the divine love within you and all around you to radiate from you and to work through you. Notice how you view the world with so much more curiosity and joy! Notice how much more fun you have! Notice the level of connection you feel! Notice the awe, the wonder, the beauty, the ecstasy, the joy! This is what it feels like to be in the energy of receiving. This is how the knowing drops in, the gifts turn on, and your physical body returns to a state of ease and flow. Then, it can recalibrate and harmonize to your higher frequency. The key is allowing the body to recalibrate to this higher frequency, for your physical body wants to catch up! This is about getting out of your own way and releasing the blocks. You might feel the pushback from those around you.

You might feel the judgments and perceptions. These are not yours. This is where their limiting beliefs and illusory stories will bump up against your love. When you hold that frequency and meet them there, those energies have the opportunity to be transmuted, and those wounds have the opportunity to be healed. But when you give in to the projections, the stories, and the old ways of being, you are not living as love.

Be love. Notice the lightness you feel as you release judgment and comparison. As you honor the beauty and gifts available all around you. As you celebrate one another, and thus open the space for all to access more. As you realize you are all one, you will also realize that living as love is the only way to truly tap into the higher collective knowledge. Living in division has created weakness in the field. When you come together in unity, as love, this is a force that cannot be stopped. It is the force of healing, of transmutation, of new worlds, and of infinite possibilities. To choose to be love ends the division. As each person radiates love and comes together with others as love, the light is so strong and the momentum so fierce that this is the only way forward, and nothing can push you off your highest path.

Wherever you have resistance to giving and receiving love is the place to look. Where do you block yourself from fully receiving love? This is where you live in illusions of what you do and don't deserve. You are from love. You are love. You are endlessly deserving of it. You need not do anything to receive it and be worthy of it. Nothing changes your worthiness. Allow yourself to live in the infinite worthiness of love, for there are forces all around that want to pour love into you. The love within you wants to be seen, to be acknowledged, and to grow. Surrender to it. Allow others to see you—the true you. Allow others to give you love and to nourish you. Where do you block your own nourishment?

Love is the life force that heals. It is the ultimate medicine and the ultimate activator. It is how you anchor into ascension. Allow the divine to love you. Allow divine love to flow through you. To not is to live in illusion. Living as truth is living as love. Receiving love is the natural flow of things—the cycle of giving and receiving, all to be in balance. The more you allow yourself to receive love, you will also feel your capacity to give love and be love increase, and thus you all work together to add more momentum to the path of love for all.

Where you believe you are not worthy of love is where you are in illusion. Decide to break through. Decide to live your truth. It is when you live as love, giving and receiving it, that you align with ascension. You allow it to move you forward, you allow yourself to receive wisdom, you allow yourself to receive higher guidance, you allow yourself to receive signs, you allow yourself to receive lessons, you allow yourself to receive joy, and this is how you experience what you have always desired. Get out of your own way! Love isn't about what your ego wants—it's about what your soul needs. It's about what your soul knows, because your soul is love. It is time for this to be fully expressed.

It is love that allows you to see truth and be truth. When you live as love, truth is the only way.

TABLET VII: PEACE

Peace is your guide to the highest state of alignment, where you are walking the path of love and truth. Lack of peace will direct you to where you are not living in alignment with truth, and thus where you are not aligned with pure love—your divine essence.

Here we come to the Tablet of Peace—peace naturally following the codes of truth and love. For when you live as love, and when you live your truth, peace naturally follows. It is not something that you must find—it is something that you are. How can you embody peace? This is a state of flow, a state of ease, moving through you. It is Source, pure love, flowing through you, that resonates as peace within the system. Anywhere there is not peace within the system points to where you are out of alignment with truth—out of alignment with the Highest truth of your divinity, the Highest truth of Source, the Highest truth of love. Anything other than peace is your roadmap to realigning with peace, for aligning with the feeling of peace is how you know you are living your truth. It is discord, it is nonresonance, and it is upset that show you where you are not fully embodying love.

What brings you out of your peace? What aligns you with peace? When you are aligned with truth, this knowing is clear. Let us focus on the former question—what brings you out of your peace? It is trust in yourself that allows you to see this truth and to know this truth, but you must be willing to fully live in truth for it to be seen and known clearly within you. Otherwise, you block yourself from the knowing. It is not that you do not know what brings you out of your peace—it is that you fear releasing it. It is that you fear what is on the other side. You fear upsetting something or someone, you fear betting on yourself, you fear that something better will not come along, or you fear it will not work out. So I ask you—do you believe it is true that you must live out of alignment with peace and love for the rest of your life? Is this what you believe you are destined for? Is this what you believe you are meant for? Do you believe living out of alignment with your peace will somehow lead you to a destination that is peace?

The road to peace is peace. It is not somewhere you will get—it is a way you will be, and you can choose this way of being now. Where are you betraying your own peace because you believe that choosing your peace will make others uncomfortable or upset them? You must be willing to shift the status quo. You must be willing to stand up for your own peace if you are to bring the frequency of peace to this world.

This is what you are here to do. You must live in your peace to spread the code of peace for others to feel, which then unlocks it within them as well. When others feel you living the code of peace, it unlocks their own remembrance that peace is the way, a natural byproduct of love, and a remarkably helpful indicator of where you are not living in alignment with love. Specifically, it is a helpful indicator of where you are living out of alignment with love for yourself, from which all else comes. Allow yourself to anchor into truth, and allow yourself to see—what is bringing you out of your peace?

It might be a relationship, it might be a thought, it might be a pattern, a habit, an activity, a piece of your career, your whole career, a way of being, or an obligation. Why is it an obligation? Where have you decided you are obligated to anything? This is where you have forgotten your highest truth—your greatest gift of free will, of choice. Where you are living in the illusion that you are obligated to anything or anyone is where you are giving your power away, where you have forgotten your power, and where you are living in the illusion that you do not have choice. To give your choice away is also a choice. When you live in the illusion that you have no choice, and that you must live in obligation, this is where you block the expansion of the codes. This is where you blunt your magnetism. This is where you anchor yourself to lower frequencies. This is where you are tied to illusion itself, inherently unaligned with your truth. To dedicate yourself to truth is a choice, and you must consistently choose this to anchor into the higher frequencies, to keep choosing the path of ascension, to expand your consciousness, and to see what you are truly capable of.

You are always choosing. Commitment is consistent choice. And so, are you consistently choosing truth? Are you consistently choosing love? Are you consistently choosing peace? Or are you choosing truth once, and then choosing obligation? Are you choosing truth once, and then choosing to abdicate responsibility? You must choose responsibility if you wish to anchor into ascension. There is no more hiding. You are meant for peace. What is taking you out of your peace? See this. Face this. And then, to align with your peace, what is the choice? This is what you know. Observe what is taking you out of your peace, or rather, what you are allowing to take you out of your peace, one by one, and notice the choices. Get curious—why and how is it taking you out of your peace? Is it because the thing itself is not in alignment? Or is it your relationship with it? Is it how you're showing up to it? Are you projecting your own assumptions and expectations onto it?

Before making a choice, if you wish to see in truth, you must allow the shifting of perception. Shift your perception as many ways as you can in order to see the multidimensionality of it all. This is what you might refer to as "playing devil's advocate." It is to explore every side, neutrally. This is another place where you are invited to take responsibility—where have you been taking yourself out of your own peace? How have you been keeping yourself from peace? For it is only you who can keep you from your peace—not another. It is not always about what is in your reality, but rather your relationship with it.

You will find that when you choose peace—when nothing is able to disturb you from your peace—you feel a state of enlightenment. You are consistently in flow, and this is where you have fully unlocked the ascension code of truth. Peace is a helpful barometer. Be brave. Choose your peace. Use your lack of peace as another guiding light—what is underneath this? What choices are you making that keep you from peace? When you align with love, you know that you are meant for peace. To live your divinity is to be in peace, and to be peace. Love is peaceful. Truth creates peace. It is where you stay in illusions and where you compromise your values and your truth that you feel disruption, and chaos follows.

Can you imagine a world where you live in peace? This is on its way, but you must create this experience. It will require you to choose peace. It will require you to choose another way to respond, a different way than you have before. It will require you to speak up for truth and to embody truth. It will require you to live as love and live with forgiveness. And so, will you choose peace over ego? Will you choose peace over anger? Will you choose peace over drama? Will you choose the ascended Earth—the New Earth that you crave? Will you choose this over the temptation of what you are used to and over the temptations of the ego? It is up to you. It is consistent dedication to your ascension. It is consistently choosing love and truth that brings you peace.

You might reflect on what *does* bring you peace. How good does that feel, simply to think about it? The simple, peaceful moments! You will realize that nothing grandiose is necessary for you to feel peace. Much of what you believe brings you happiness is actually just a momentary rush of endorphins—is this true happiness? Or a moment of instant gratification? Excitement? An addiction? Peace is a state of being that you are meant to align with. When you think of what feels peaceful, what is that for you? The gentle crash of ocean waves, the salty air by the ocean, the sand beneath your toes. The chirps of the birds, the warmth of the sun's rays on your skin, the crisp autumn air, the fresh smell of pine trees in the forest. The laughter with friends, the tender touch of a lover, the hug of a loved one. A deep breath. Silence. Stillness. Being.

What is peace to you?

What would it look like for you to dedicate your way of being to peace? As a state? For you to bring peace to everything you do? This allows you to flow instead of force. When you live emitting the vibration of peace, it allows you to see more clearly. It allows you to access multidimensionality. You are not reactive. You are present. You are fully receiving every single moment. You access your inner wisdom. You embody your divinity. You emanate a calmness to all around you. The energy softens, the moment opens, and you unlock these codes of peace for others not by trying, but by simply being. What would your life look like if you were to live peace?

Many might feel a jolt of fear or concern as they realize how out of alignment with peace they are. The fear of what might need to be released! You ask, *but how will I get anything done?* Why can you not be productive from a state of peace? In fact, it is the most productive state to approach any situation from, for the frequency is a natural amplifier of energy. It naturally opens and expands energy fields. It lightens the vibrational undertone of any experience. It calms it down. It transmutes chaos to direct flow. This is the power of peace. Notice how in the codes themselves you feel yourself getting out of peace when you run to your mind. From this you might realize where your mind takes you out of peace based on conditioning, questions, assumptions, and staying busy in your brain. This is not your soul. It is a process for your system.

But when you anchor into your divinity, when you anchor into your soul, when you live, choose, and explore from the truth of your soul, and when your intuition fully guides you, peace is natural. Your intuition is always guiding you along the path of love, and this is your path of peace. It is one step at a time, one moment at a time, and one choice at a time. How can you bring peace to everything you do? How can you move through life from the frequency of peace? How can you breathe peace into every interaction and every experience? You feel the peace in your body as you read this! You feel the peace in your body as you invite this way of being in, because it is liberation! Because it is you choosing to unchain yourself from the energy of obligation. Because it is you choosing creation—to be the creator, to step into your gifts fully, and to bring spiritual mastery to everything you do. This is living from the divine state.

This is what you are here to do—to remember your truth, and to live from truth, instead of living from programs. This is waking up to your truth. It is holding a higher state of being. It will take living in this new way dutifully, with commitment, that will allow the general state of amnesia to dissolve more effortlessly for others. It is time to break apart the lower frequencies bit by bit, and this begins with you. It is the voice of a child when one stamps their feet and complains that they just want to do what everyone else is doing. It is the unevolved mind that does not explore for itself and does not invite in a higher state of seeing, being, living, and knowing. I say this clearly so you can address the parts of you that resist embodying love and forgiveness, the parts that resist living with peace. Do you feel that—where you resist your own peace? Where do you believe it's "easier" to live another way? Easier because others are doing it, but then what are you creating? What do you want to take responsibility for? What is the legacy you wish to live out? Now is the time to choose—how will you leave this experience? How will you live this experience?

You have been guided to these tablets to unlock your soul's evolution. To integrate your spiritual mastery. To live with the mastery that is available to you—not to be controlled by programs. To live in an awakened state. To bring the higher codes of consciousness into everything you do. This is how you shift the overall frequency of the planet. And so, I invite you to step into these higher codes. I invite you to claim your divinity, and to live as love. To live with peace. To take ownership of where you are not, and allow yourself to choose differently. This is the only way you will identify what is out of alignment with you living as love, living your joy, and living your excitement, which are the path to your spiritual mastery.

You must recognize where you are and are not in peace. You must choose to infuse your lives with peace and to follow peace. This is not always the "easier" decision for the ego, but it is the conscious decision of the awakened one, of the one who is living from their divine essence as love, and of the one who is ready to bring the higher codes of consciousness to this world.

Allow peace. It is spacious. It opens. It opens your energy, it opens the field, and it attracts in more of the same. It is expansive. Suddenly it becomes clear where you are not choosing peace. Choosing peace for one will look different than for another, for the frequency is felt individually. It is alignment with peace that allows you to find your natural flow and rhythm, and it takes many rhythms harmonizing together to create the song of the universe. The collective song of the soul—what is your rhythm within it? What is your flow? Some will be slower, some faster, some consistent, and some more varied. Your peace will not look like another's.

Where you are worried about others and what they are doing, judging how they are living and being, and deciding for them if they are living in or out of peace is where you are out of alignment with peace itself. Can you live in the peace that all are fulfilling their contracts exactly as they are meant to? That all are moving through their own lessons for their highest soul evolution exactly as they must? That what you can control is yourself? And you bring peace. To judge others and to worry about others is where you are not choosing peace.

Notice where your ego and your brain start to wander off into staying busy and into avoidance. Underneath this is where you can learn what the limiting beliefs, programs, and illusions are that you have been unknowingly buying into and living from. Allow yourself to bring to the surface all of the reasons you are telling yourself you cannot choose peace and all of the resistance you have to the idea. Simply explore it. This is the gold! The gold is where you can bring so clearly to the surface what is holding you back, where there has been fear, guilt, shame, and judgment threaded into your operating system, threaded into your rulebooks, and threaded into your society through what has been normalized. It is only in bringing this to the surface, facing it head-on, and exploring how it is out of alignment with truth and peace that you can start to rewrite the story.

This is part of your duty as an upholder of the codes—to rewrite the story for yourself, in alignment with love, truth, and peace, and to live as this embodiment. From there, others can naturally follow the codes. You start to see how you have been following a separate set of codes, systems, and rules, but never consciously opted in, and you do not know exactly what those codes are, yet you have been living by them! This is how they have been so insidiously threaded into your way of being. This is the nonresonance. This is the lack of peace you feel in your system—where you have taken on rules or ideas from another that are not in alignment with your divinity. So this comes to the surface. This comes to conscious awareness to be faced, to be cleared, and to be rewritten, and now you live as your truth again.

I recognize that you will find resistance. I recognize that many of you will gloss over this as "easier said than done," or "I already know this." Oh, dear one, when it is "easier said than done," is that way of thinking not what has gotten your collective stuck in the first place? From that way of thinking, you are not taking responsibility for shifting the mold. From that way of thinking, you are not taking responsibility for creating new grooves of what is "normal," and choosing grooves that align with peace. It is a choice to pave a new way. Those who jump to "I already know this" are, in fact, those who are not living it. The one who lives their divinity lives with curiosity and openness and is always willing to hear the high codes of truth as many times as possible, for each time unlocks a new layer of knowing and experience. It is a sneaky form of resistance—to gloss over it by thinking you already know it. This is where you do not want to look at it. To live your divinity is to live as the student, which unlocks your mastery.

What other codes bring this up for you? There is always more to unlock—more codes within the frequency of the phrase or the idea. You simply have to allow them in. To those who gloss over them in any which way, are you willing to claim that you are fully living these codes? In their purest form? Those who are will be ready to fully receive every word, every phrase, every idea, every concept, and every packet of knowledge, for they do not live in fear—they live in truth. To live in truth is to allow yourself to see all. To look at it directly. To be fully present and focused on what is in front of you. It is only then that you can discern clearly. Where you want to jump ahead is where you are avoiding something. What is it that you are avoiding?

This you know in your heart.

Allow peace to be your guiding light. Yes, it can be peaceful! Yes, you can choose peace! Choosing love creates peace. You will find that as you dedicate yourself to true peace, you will naturally choose love and forgiveness. You must live truth, see truth, and speak truth to be in pure peace. Spend more time in this frequency. Prioritize your peace and watch as your frequency shifts. Watch as you magnetize your desires. Watch as your inner knowing—the wisdom that is already within your cells, waiting to be unlocked—bursts open effortlessly. Notice as you tap into your highest potential, as you fully receive life and all it has to offer you, as what you have been seeking seeks you, and as what you have been seeking moves through you. This is the gift of peace—a gift you can choose for yourself. Peace opens the space, opens the energy, and allows more love to move through and expand out. This is your code of peace.

TABLET VIII: CHANGE AND MATURITY

To live truth is to live in the flow. To live truth is to be in the constant change of all, as this is your natural state. To commit to your truth and to living as love, you must allow for change. It is the integration of truth, of wisdom, and of the many lessons you are gifted that is maturity—the embodiment of your wisdom. In allowing change and maturity, you dedicate yourself to the ascension journey, and you commit to the allowance of truth as you know it to continue to expand.

We arrive at the last tablet—the Tablet of Change and Maturity, the codes that will allow you to live in a state of expansion, and a reminder of what is available to you. Change is a natural state. To flow, to expand, to learn, and to change—this is a natural state when you are aligned with truth and when you are committed to expansion. To consistently embody and access more of your multidimensionality inherently requires change. To live in your flow, to live in your curiosity, inherently is to live in a state of change. And so, where do you resist change? Where do you cling so tightly to the way things are, or the way they were, yet you also desire something different? You desire something better, yet you will not let go. This is how you chain yourself, anchoring yourself to ways that are more difficult.

To commit to your truth is to also commit to change, for committing to your truth is allowing yourself to see new ways, new ideas, new memories, and new wisdom. Although I say "new," it is not that they are truly "new" overall, but rather "new" in this experience for you, "new" in being explored at this time and in this way. It is remembering. It is accessing what feels new but has really always been there. It has been waiting to be seen, like an old coat you notice for the first time in your closet. For ease of communication, I will employ the word "new," but understand it is not truly "new" at all, just at this point being consciously accessed and brought to the forefront.

As you are in a state of exploration and curiosity—as you honor your truth—you are consistently bringing things to conscious awareness, and your truth expands. For truth is far more in alignment with change than stuckness, despite what many believe. Remember that truth is a frequency. The key is following this energy. What resonated as truth for you before might not anymore, as your frequency has shifted, as other pockets of vibration have been unlocked within you, and as new experiences have been uncovered. And so, what is in alignment for you as this more expanded version of you? What is in alignment with you as the purest expression of yourself, mixed with the new frequencies that are available in the collective, or according to what you perceive to be time, the season, your location, and so on?

For example, let's assume you are living at your purest, most authentic frequency, and let's call this frequency yellow. Let's say that your purest frequency is mixed with the vibration of a certain location you're visiting, or a certain friend, or a certain time of year, and let's say any of those examples is vibrating at the frequency of blue. And so, together you create green. But perhaps you switch locations, or spend time with another being, or change your diet, or the season changes, and let's say any of those shifts is vibrating at the frequency of red. Now, you create orange. Thus, the truth of what is naturally shifts—this is the only way. The natural flow of things is change, is movement, and you feel this when you notice that anything that feels stuck feels like resistance. Flow is movement. Things that never change feel stuck because your inner knowing, your inner wisdom, knows that change is the natural flow. This state of flow is guiding you to uncovering new pockets of wisdom and more aspects of yourself—this is the exploration! This is the excitement! This is what you signed up for in this experience!

There is always much to learn! That is part of the fun of it all! Because there are so many frequencies of information and experience to potentially tap into, the opportunities are endless! When you stay in a chronic state of stuckness, when there is no movement, you start to feel the colors dull, you feel things slow down, you feel heavy, and you feel sluggish. Your body is always moving. There is always internal movement—as you breathe, blood pumps through your body, you digest, neurons fire, and so on. Nature is always in a state of movement. That which appears to be still is in fact a collection of vibrating molecules, constantly shifting. To live in the quantum state is to live in flow and to live in movement—and where will that lead you? That is the fun! That is the joy! When you are living truth, you live in flow, and you live with movement.

If you are committed to not changing, you are choosing resistance. If you are committed to not changing, you are committed to staying in limitation. To choose truth is to choose exploration and curiosity. It is to choose honesty. If you are committed to nothing changing, how could you fully allow honesty in your life—with others and yourself? Sometimes perceptions shift, and sometimes feelings shift, for the natural state of energy is to flow. Whether the frequency intensifies and deepens, or if it changes to something entirely different, there is movement. If you are attached to nothing changing, you will not honor this flow of energy. You will not honor your truth as you outgrow things. You will not honor your truth as feelings shift. You will not honor the truths that must be looked at for you to live in peace, and for you to live as love.

I will be quite clear: to live truth, to uphold this code, to live this code, you must always allow for change. This is the expansion. It is not growth for the sake of growth. It is allowing the container to remain open. It is allowing fluidity—to honor all of yourself, to invite more in, to allow the entire journey to unfold rather than get stuck at one destination. It is the accumulation of experiences, emotions, and lessons that all continuously add together that allow you to deepen your understanding of yourself, of the universe, and of your divinity. It is ever-growing and expanding, for it is all. The Source is all—it is endless. It is unlimited. You are an extension of this. Love is endless. It is unlimited. It is an endless source. And so, to allow this to flow through you is to allow yourself to be without limitation. To uncap yourself. To allow the movement, the deepening, the expansion, the growth, and the uncovering.

This is how you tap into the richness of life, and the richness of the lessons it has to offer. This is how you juice the most out of every lemon, because you allow yourself to take any single encounter, experience, or thought and fully uncap its potential. That "one" is an extension of the unlimited source, and so, when you uncap it, you allow the endless energies connected to it and moving through it to flow through, and from that "one" you access the infinite, if you allow yourself to. You do not need to move onto the next to always experience "more." Realize there can always be "more" if you allow yourself to sink into the infinite possibilities of any single point, that is not a point at all, but rather movement within the flow of all, connected to all, a portal to all.

You might return to this text endless times and read something different each time. You might return to the same sunset at the beach every day and have a new feeling, a new insight, and a new experience. You might return to the same quote and access more from it each time. You might return to the same friend, to the same conversation, and unlock a new experience every time. Because it's never really the same. And so, the natural state is learning, being in awareness of the change, and accessing more. For if you are committed to embodying love and divinity, you are aligned with truth, you are aligned with unlimited possibilities, and you are aligned with the infinite. The oneness that unlocks the infinite. What a beautiful place to be!

Recognize that things will change. You will change. You will uncover and embody more of yourself. What is your relationship with change? In what ways do you fear change? Why do you cling to the old? It is your ego that clings to the old. It is your fear that clings to what is familiar, simply because what is unfamiliar could be dangerous, from the perspective of the ego, but from the perspective of the soul is where you access more of the One—more of yourself. Trust yourself. Trust your soul. And so, you understand more of how fear is controlling your decisions, and how when you align with love instead of fear, you release the resistance to change. You allow things to flow and shift and realign as they are meant to for your highest soul evolution. You understand that when you return back to what you knew before, it is not really what you knew before, but actually an entirely new experience of the same thing. You are not the same person you were one moment ago! Can you allow this?

Allow yourself to make new decisions and to see from a new perspective. Who does it serve to stay the way you were, if it no longer resonates for you? It serves the expectations of others and the fear of others, because it makes them feel as though they know what to expect. This is the illusory comfort of the ego. And so, I ask you, are you here to serve their ego, or to serve the highest truth? To serve the ego, or to live as love? As more of you flow within the change, become comfortable with change, and invite in new systems and ways of being with the underlying knowing that those as well must be allowed to shift and change, it will open up space for others to understand they need not fear what is not permanent. In fact, this is how they access more freedom. You start to uncover where you have unintentionally been choosing the opposite of freedom as a desperate attempt to feel safety, and how it has not, in fact, created what you desired.

More of you are becoming more and more repulsed by the idea of stagnancy. More of you feel the internal knowing that being locked in to one way of being, one way of doing, one way of thinking, or one identity does not feel right in your system. This is part of ascension, because you are aligned with the truth, so you are aligned with change, and you have remembered the liberation in allowing yourself to live in the flow, which inherently changes. You will notice the energetic tug of any people, systems, structures, or ways of being that are designed to keep you stagnant and block you from learning and growing, or from outgrowing what is.

Notice this, and you will be able to bring in new ways and new structures that are in fact designed to facilitate growth and align with flow. For if the systems are not designed to change, they are not efficient systems at all. But so much of how your society has been set up and how you have been taught to create safety has been to create things that align with permanence so you know what to expect and so you know what to do. But then you outgrow it. And then, what next? You stay in systems and structures and ways of being and doing that you have outgrown, for the sake of not rocking the boat, but you have outgrown it all so much that there is discord, and then it falls apart. It is like a child growing four shoe sizes and trying to force their foot in the old shoe. This only leads to pain and suffering. It only leads to suffocation. As you design your life, as you make your choices, as you move forward, are you setting up systems that support your growth and expansion? Or are you accidentally setting up systems that block your expansion? That anchor you into one hobby or activity or way of being? The only thing that can anchor you down is you. This is where you can decide to shift your desires and to shift your life choices—this is part of the expansion and ascension.

Notice how it triggers others when you make even the slightest of changes—changing your diet, starting a new routine, changing the way in which you interact with others, saying no when you usually say yes, or even changing your hairstyle. Notice how people are used to commenting about it. Notice how they might not even understand why they are resistant to seeing the change. It is because they are afraid of change themselves. They are afraid because they are taught to be, not because it is their highest truth. When you understand that change is actually your freedom, when you remember this wisdom—that you are allowed to be all, and that you are meant to shift within your many forms—now you can take a sigh of relief.

What is consistent is meant to be from choice, not from obligation. And so, how do you release yourself from the chains of obligation? You allow yourself the permission to change. This change is not for the sake of change. It allows spaciousness. It allows for movement and flow as it feels aligned. It is the space to follow alignment. So many do not follow their truth, do not choose truth, do not choose peace, and do not follow alignment because they have boxed themselves in through deciding that they cannot change. And who is that from? How does that serve you? Do you see how you limit yourself? What would it look like for you to unlimit yourself, and to let yourself flow?

The high code of truth is change, because it is only through living within the energy of change that you can allow yourself to access a higher frequency, that you can allow yourself to flow, that you give yourself the room to always live your truth. Understand that these truths can shift, they will be expressed differently, and you will consistently uncover more wisdom that is within you. Perhaps things might feel consistent or similar—this is all and well, but that will be coming from natural alignment, rather than forcing them to stay the same. You cannot force natural change. It is a powerful, beautiful, natural force that moves through you and moves around you. It is the divine working her magic in this world. You will never be bored with her!

Committing to ascension is committing to change—changing perceptions, allowing paradigms to shift, and allowing desires and habits to shift. You become clearer and clearer on what feels good for you in the now. You become clear on what is truly expanding you, what is holding you down, what is keeping you stagnant, and what is limiting you. If you are committed to holding your previous worldview, you are not living ascension. This process will expand your mind and your consciousness. This expansion is change! This process will surprise you. It will push you. It will stretch you. It will ask you to release all that is serving your ego but not your soul. It will ask you to always stay in the present and honor the truth of the now, instead of the truth of what once was. It will require you to consistently recalibrate your field to the highest truth, to the highest alignment, and to the highest of frequencies. It will consistently recalibrate you, and thus your external reality shifts.

If you are in your own way and you choose to block this recalibration, dis-ease will present. It will not feel good. You will see physical manifestations of the resistance. Through ascension, your mind will change, your frequency will change, your body will change, your worldviews will change, your desires will change, your enjoyments will change, and you will live as change. You will create change naturally, simply by living in your truth and allowing this to be updated consistently. It is moment to moment, present awareness. It is allowing yourself to observe what once was serving you and now is not, to face where you have been living in illusions, to explore your shadows, to explore your depths, and to explore ideas that others are too afraid to see. It is all in what appears to be darkness. Do you dare venture there? The path of ascension is change. It is unlocking the change within you. As this occurs, it unlocks the change in your world.

With change is maturity. Allowing the flower to mature to bloom. Allowing the fine wine to mature to its optimal taste. Allowing your perceptions to mature. Allowing yourself to mature. I invite you to release whatever associations you might have with the word "maturing." Maturing is not giving up your fun or your play! It is allowing change. It is allowing wisdom. It is living as wisdom. It is inviting in expansion and allowing the space for this. This is maturity. Will you allow your maturity? Your growth? Why do you fear this maturity? What have you decided comes with this? As you mature and live the truth of your soul, you live in peace.

Maturity allows you to effortlessly release the illusions of obligation, the fears that come from conditioning instead of truth, and the stories and chaos that might run your mind. The maturity of your soul-led self is the embodiment of your wisdom and the embodiment of your divinity. You no longer have to create drama. You no longer have to create intense scenarios to feel a momentary surge of energy to connect you with a deeper feeling. You *are* the depth of feeling. You are aligned with the deepest, most divine feelings of ecstasy—pure love, pure peace, and pure truth. There is no need to concoct scenarios riddled with drama or fear to bring up these emotions, because the richness of love is always available to you. It is moving through you. You are embodying this.

What many do not realize is that they choose to stay in their lower levels of consciousness. They choose to resist change, they choose to live in fear and scarcity and create more drama in their lives because they are seeking the intensity of emotion, they are looking to create something of meaning, they are looking to connect with something greater than themselves, they are looking for movement and change so it feels like something is happening. This is a wounded manifestation of creatorship. It is like trying to paint a masterpiece with your toes instead of using your hands. Instead, what if you allowed yourself to live in trust? Allow yourself to embody your divinity and to access your spiritual mastery through living as love and forgiveness. From there, you will tap into the richest, most delicious experiences of all. You will constantly be floating in a sea of love and peace, the unlimited source. Instead of searching for a momentary surge of energy, you are always flowing with its movement. You are in the sea of unlimited love. And so, the drama is unnecessary, and the illusions are unnecessary—for the sea of love and the alignment with truth always guide you to the next, as this is the natural state of change. You feel the movement, and you are satisfied.

This code of maturity also involves responsibility. As you access greater gifts, as you unlock more potential within yourself, you must use your wisdom and inner power with maturity and responsibility. The key is to not revert back to your ego. If you are feeling stuck in your ascension journey, you must look with honesty at yourself and see where you might have fallen out of maturity. It is not whether or not you are deserving. It is whether or not you are aligned with the vibration of ascension and spiritual mastery. It is an energetic calibration. Where you are not aligned with your maturity, where you are not in responsibility, you may have fallen out of alignment with higher ascension, and the codes cannot be unlocked within you, for you are not embodying the key. The key is a vibration. This cannot be faked.

You can tell yourself in your mind whatever you please, but energy is clear. Whatever is occurring is a reflection of your energy, even if you tell yourself something else is going on. This is where anchoring into honesty always keeps you in the light of truth. There might be times when you feel as though you cannot see what you need to. When you feel like you're in the dark, ask yourself when you stepped into it. What would it take for you to step into the light of truth? The willingness to uphold the higher codes of truth. The willingness to see truth. The willingness to allow maturity and change. The willingness to choose love in all moments. The willingness to be present to what is in your present. This process of ascension, these codes of truth, to live these White Tablets, to access your ascension and highest learning will require a higher maturity within you. It is up to you to choose it. If you don't, it is the wise being who will ask themselves why, who will ask themselves where the resistance comes from, and who will ask themselves what they are afraid of. Once again, it brings you to truth.

This final tablet unlocks the codes of change and maturity, for it is change that allows for maturity, and it is maturity that is the integration of the wisdom within and the embodiment of truth. It is full integration of all of yourself, of the knowledge from your experiences, of your inner wisdom, of the love that moves through you, and of the divinity within you that is the unlocking of yourself as infinite possibility. This is the process of ascension. It is a journey that consistently expands you. It is a journey that consistently invites you to more—more curiosity, more exploration, more love, and more wisdom. Will you accept this invitation? Only you can decide.

CONCLUSION

To witness these tablets is to unlock your inner knowing and your remembrance of what you are here to do. You are not here to stay stagnant, loved one. You are not here to stay small. You are here to live your truth, and that vibration is vast, it is powerful, it is ever-growing and changing, and it is that which moves you to other dimensions, other planes of being, and other levels of consciousness. It is a divine force—truth. It is what releases you from the illusions of limitation. As you live the codes and are conscious of these ways of being in your daily life, you will notice as you unlock new frequencies. You will notice as your external reality recalibrates. These codes— to be in their vibration, to read them, to witness them, to soak them in—unlock the lessons that are critical for your individual soul evolution to fully unravel. The process of spiritual mastery and of accessing your highest gifts is waiting for you, but it is up to you to choose it. It requires more of you. It requires you to live in your truth. It requires you to live most authentically as your divine self.

You will notice where fear runs the show and where the illusion that you are separate from the divine, that you are separate from Source, shows up in your life. You will notice where you have been living out of alignment with truth. Your reality will recalibrate so you attract experiences, teachers, thoughts, and gifts that support you in ascension. This process is energetic, it is physical, and it is emotional—it spans all planes. You will change. It requires courage to consistently choose truth. To choose ascension. To choose love. This is something you decide, and all energies aligned with this support you in it. You have master teachers all around, and a divine teacher within you. It is from this divine teacher that you access infinite wisdom. You are infinitely connected. The wisdom is within you. The question is—will you dedicate yourself to unlocking it?

As you do, your body will shift. Old emotions will release. New emotions will move through. You will access depth. You will become more sensitive because you are no longer living in the dark. You are in the light of truth. Are you ready to feel this frequency? Are you ready to shine the light of truth fully on yourself? You might feel as though this is vulnerable—to fully expose truth. It is to be energetically naked, but is it not more vulnerable to live in falsities? To live in illusions? For when the truth rises, as it will, and it hits you on the side of the head, you will feel blindsided. The truth always rises. At this time, the truth is coming through swiftly, fiercely, lovingly, and powerfully. You can either realign with this ascension wave or you can choose not to. But it will in fact feel like more resistance to fight it, because it is the natural flow of things to ride this wave.

You will recognize that the only way to truly move forward and honor yourself, to be in integrity, to choose truth, and to choose love for yourself is to no longer betray yourself. Do not turn your back on yourself. Do not keep your divinity in the darkness. Dedicate yourself to unlocking and living your deep wisdom, to allowing yourself to be the student, and to living in curiosity. When you choose this path of ascension, the rewards are unlimited. There is unlimited love around you and within you, supporting you—but it is up to you to choose to align with it. This will be a breath of fresh air! This is your peace—to live this love, and to receive this love. To live in the light of the truth. To break free from what is nonresonant, that which is not truth. What is not truth—what is not authentic—is not a sturdy foundation. It is limited. It will not survive the shift that is occurring.

Now is your moment to choose yourself. To choose the truest version of yourself. To choose your divine wisdom, your spiritual mastery, and your ascension. To choose truth. As you embody these codes and as you uphold these codes in your own life, you unlock faster ascension for all. When you calibrate to the highest timeline for all and you anchor in the highest light of truth, more energy is added to the new reality that is fully aligned with truth, love, and peace. Step into your truth with pride and with love.

Living truth is the highest code of ascension that unlocks all. Unlock the path of ascension, and consistently choose it. This is through being love, through living with integrity, through choosing peace, through forgiveness, through surrender, through divine responsibility, through trust in the process, through the allowance of change, and through the integration of your wisdom. From this, your frequency recalibrates, your external reality recalibrates, and you unlock the next door on your journey of ascension, of uncovering your divine gifts, and of living the highest truth. Truth is the key.

It is the surrendered student of the White Tablets who lives as the master of ascension—the living embodiment of divine love.

ABOUT THE AUTHOR

Christina Rice is an intuitive channel, celebrity energy healer, best-selling author, and founder of Ahai 7D Energy Healing. Her mission is to support freedom-seekers in stepping into their power, creating their dream realities, and living their most authentic, abundant, and aligned lives. Christina works as a bridge between realms, sharing transformational channeled messages from a number of different Ascended Masters and teaching others how to work with energy to create lasting change in their lives.

Christina has helped thousands of people master the energetics of money, health, and relationships through her books, membership, in-person immersions, and powerful online programs. She is the host of her own podcast, Christina the Channel, and founder of QRTZ, a spiritual lifestyle brand offering high-vibe products for your everyday life. She also supports other leaders in sharing their own paradigm-shifting messages and stories through her publishing house, Golden Hour Publishing. You can find more from Christina at www. christinathechannel.com.

DIVE DEEPER
WITH CHRISTINA

Manifestation Mastery: How to Shift Your Reality & Co-Create with the Universe

Manifestation Mastery: How to Shift Your Reality & Co-Create with the Universe will help you move past the limiting beliefs keeping you stuck, access your inner truth, and become a magnet for everyday miracles. This best-selling book is a trance channeled text from an energy called the Monarch Being, which Christina experiences as a stream of divine feminine and divine masculine consciousness. In this text, the Monarch Being explains the energetics of manifestation and how to fully step into your power as a co-creator of your own reality. Their goal is to empower each individual to be the leader in their own lives, to create a life where they truly feel free, and to reconnect with their true essence as an extension of Source.

Get your copy at ***manifestationmasterybook.com***.

Pain, Love, & Purpose

Pain, Love, & Purpose is a collection of poems about moments that define us. This book contains 143 poems separated into three sections–pain, love, and purpose–that detail the relationships, emotions, and experiences that have been part of Christina's own journey turning her pain into her purpose. This book helps us understand that while we might not all have the same experiences, we can find deep connection with each other through shared emotions. This collection of poetry offers a reflection for each reader to perceive their own moments of pain, love, and purpose with a new perspective, and to see how those experiences ultimately guide us to our inner truth.

Get your copy at ***painloveandpurpose.com***.

5D Ascension Activator Free Online Course

5D Ascension
Activator Free
Course

*30 Channeled Messages to
Shift to 5D*

If you're ready to raise your vibration and amplify your manifestation practice, this is for you!

In this free course, Christina shares 30 trance channeled messages from different Ascended Masters and Light Beings to help you shift to 5D consciousness and align with abundance and miracles. Each channeled lesson also comes with corresponding journal prompts, action steps, and a deeper explanation from Christina to help you integrate the messages and truly make the shift to 5D.

Enroll for free at *bit.ly/5dactivator.*

Daily Manifestation Meditation

This powerful fifteen-minute meditation will help you raise your frequency and supercharge your manifestation practice! Use it daily for accelerated results.

```
Manifestation
Meditation

Become a
Manifestation Magnet!
```

Get the free meditation at *bit.ly/ctcmanifestationmeditation.*